USING PSYCHOLOGY IN BUSINESS

For Anna and Miranda

Using Psychology in Business

A Practical Guide for Managers

Mark Parkinson

Gower

Published by
Gower Publishing Limited
Gower House
Croft Road
Aldershot
Hampshire GU11 3HR
England

Gower
Old Post Road
Brookfield
Vermont 05036
USA

British Library Cataloguing in Publication Data
Parkinson, Mark
    Using psychology in business : a practical guide for
    managers
    1. Psychology, Industrial   2. Management – Psychological
    aspects
    I. Title
    158.7

    ISBN 0 566 08129 6

Library of Congress Cataloging-in-Publication Data
Parkinson, Mark.
    Using psychology in business: a practical guide for managers/
    Mark Parkinson.
        p.   cm.
    Includes index.
    ISBN 0–566–08129–6 (hc.)
    1. Psychology. Industrial.   2. Organizational behavior.
    I. Title.
    HF5548.8.P263   1999
    658'.001'9–dc21   99–34481
                                                                   CIP

Typeset in Sabon by IML Typographers, Chester and printed
in Great Britain by the University Press, Cambridge

Contents

consultants—Characteristics of consultants—What do
consultants do?—The project proposal—How much will
it cost?—Working out the benefits—Using consultants—
Further information

List of figures

List of tables

Preface

On a recent flight I sat next to the managing director of a large and successful company. After a while we started to talk about how psychology can improve the way in which people are managed – or, more precisely, about the application of psychological techniques to such matters as personnel selection and development. The MD said that he knew exactly what sort of people he needed to grow the business. He looked for those who were open to change, were self-starters who wanted to learn and develop new skills, and who showed initiative and a desire to take on responsibility. At a deeper level he also sought a commitment to the values and culture of the organization and a willingness to embrace a strong and positive vision of the future.

The MD, in his own enthusiastic manner, was endorsing the view that the promotion of factors such as commitment, motivation and the desire to learn have a direct link to the bottom line – in short, that good people management practices lead to stronger and more productive businesses. This is crucial insight in a world in which organizations must always aim to attract and develop high-quality staff. Indeed, making sure that you have the best processes in place for finding and keeping the right people is now a prime management requirement. It is also one that is confirmed by a growing body of research which shows that such processes have a greater impact on profitability than R&D, quality initiatives or even new technology.

This book introduces the psychological techniques that make the difference. It looks at an organization's most valuable resource – its people – and the approaches that can be used to maximize their performance. The topics covered trace a path through the exciting and rapidly growing field of business psychology. However, readers need not be concerned that the contents will be too theoretical as the aim is to show what can be done and how best to do it. As you will see, there are some interventions which must be left to professional psychologists, but there are many more which can be implemented immediately or soon after a short training programme.

Mark Parkinson
Berkshire 1999

Introduction

What is business psychology?

Business psychology is about using an understanding of human behaviour to solve problems at work. It concerns how people organize their activities and the ways in which the overall structure of work affects what they do. However, as all managers know, whatever tasks people attempt, the way in which they do them is mostly influenced by what they are like as individuals. This means that personal qualities such as ability, personality and the desire to work as one of a team are the keys to effective performance; and it is the understanding of these factors which is at the core of business psychology.

The appropriate and timely use of psychological techniques can produce significant gains in productivity at all levels in an organization. In addition, it should be emphasized that a professional analysis of the requirements of a business, and the implementation of practices which recognize and support what people have to offer, also produce a more dynamic and energized workforce – an advantage that should not be underestimated, especially in times of change. Indeed, helping organizations change, often a rather complicated process, is the primary role of the business psychologist.

Change can come in many forms and often involves a reassessment of the organization's purpose, entailing a detailed appraisal of its aims and objectives, or the introduction of new technology or working methods. All of these, in turn, are coupled with new organizational structures and changes to people's roles and responsibilities. In fact it is people 'modification' strategies that are usually at the core of all change programmes, the reason being that better people management practices are often considered to be the least disruptive way of doing things. This may or may not be true, but it is a fact that most techniques are aimed at identifying and developing the most productive employees, and making sure that they work together effectively. Thus change is driven through people in response to what is happening in the marketplace, or to technology.

The big questions

If business psychology concerns itself with people issues it is reasonable to assume that it provides the answers to a number of fundamental questions that any chief executive would expect to be informing the entire people management process – namely:

■ Do we know (precisely) what we want people to do?
■ Are we attracting and recruiting the right sort of people?
■ Are we currently employing the right range of people?
■ Are we motivating and developing people effectively?
■ Are we actively monitoring individual performance?
■ Are we encouraging people to cooperate and work together?
■ Are we making sure that people realize their full potential?
■ Are we controlling factors such as workplace stress?

These eight questions cover the three principal issues in business psychology: selection, assessment and development. For example, I have recently been involved in a large consultancy exercise for a major civil engineering company. This project required a thorough analysis of the jobs performed in all the main business units, leading to the complete specification of the requirements for each job. The information was then used to identify the most efficient ways of selecting and assessing new personnel. In addition, a number of procedures were designed that allowed for the ongoing appraisal and development of staff, with the ultimate aim of linking them to a performance-related pay system. This assignment is quite typical and serves to underline the point that interventions are aimed at integrating methods across all aspects of people management.

A plan of the book

This book provides practical advice on using a number of psychological techniques. All of them are explained with real-life examples and concentrate on showing in a straightforward way how they can benefit your organization. You will also find that there are a number of useful checklists, comments on using particular techniques, and details on sources of further information. Lastly, the psychologist's 'toolkit' is illustrated with extracts from world-class assessment tests and questionnaires.

Chapter 1 looks at how to measure and define jobs. It explores a number of job analysis methods, and addresses issues such as how to take account of jobs which incorporate multiple roles. A questionnaire is provided so that readers can perform their own analyses and generate focused job specifications. There is also an important section on competencies – the combinations of abilities, personality traits and personal skills which help profile the requirements for a job. The issue of benchmarking is then examined, alongside matters such as equality and fairness when constructing job and person specifications.

The process of recruiting and selecting staff is discussed in Chapter 2. After an introduction on how to attract suitable candidates, it looks at the use of application forms, biodata and telephone-based techniques in pre-selection. The next part looks at the selection interview and how it can be turned into a more objective way of gathering information. Different sorts of interview procedures are explained, with comments on their ease of use and applicability.

Chapter 3 focuses on psychometrics and assessment centres. There is a detailed review of psychometric tests and questionnaires, with particular emphasis given to the sorts of test used for different forms of selection and what the results mean. It includes advice on how to gain access to tests and on where to obtain the correct form of training in their use. A special section examines the problems of testing in different countries. Finally, multiple assessment procedures are described and information provided on assessment centre exercises and programmes.

Chapter 4 starts with a review of what motivates staff. It then moves on to methods of measuring motivation and the problems of retaining important personnel, paying particular attention to the issues surrounding graduate turnover. A range of strategies for retaining essential staff, such as risk analysis and modifying work patterns, are provided. The focus then changes to performance management and appraisal systems. Formal techniques such as the appraisal interview are described, with tips on what to ask and how to set objectives. There is an introduction to the latest 360-degree feedback methods and an exploration of job evaluation, or working out how much to pay employees.

Having looked at motivation and appraisal systems, Chapter 5 examines the important role of teams in organizational development. There is a review of different sorts of business teams and the characteristics of top teams. This is followed by an examination of how to build balanced teams by using approaches based on identifying team roles. The emphasis then moves to the control of management teams, with a description of different leadership styles. The chapter concludes with advice on running a team health check.

Chapter 6 concerns the strategic role of training and personal development, concentrating on ways of defining needs and maximizing the effectiveness of training. There are sections on the training 'maturity' of organizations and how to get the best out of on-the-job programmes. Advice is provided on methods of choosing and evaluating training as well as on the benefits of different sorts of individual and management development and the role of factors such as learning style. Integrated development events, and in particular the development centre, are introduced.

In Chapter 7 the issue of individual development and support is expanded by considering stress and workplace counselling – in particular, the impact of stress on work performance, and how audits and other management practices can alleviate the more common stress-related problems. The chapter then turns to the provision of counselling services and the different approaches which can be used. Importantly, it includes guidelines on the use of Employee Assistance Programmes. Next, the role which counselling has to play in outplacement and redundancy is outlined. The final section deals with international relocation and the practical problems of managing expatriate workers.

More information on the services offered by business psychologists is provided in Chapter 8. It describes the way in which they work and takes the reader through the advantages and disadvantages of employing a consultant, providing advice on matters such as the characteristics of successful consultants and methods of calculating fees and levying charges. It also gives guidance on what to expect in a project proposal, and explains how to work out the financial benefits of using various types of assessment. Lastly, there is a discussion of the different types of psychologists who work in business settings, and on how to find one to meet your needs.

At the end of the book there are some final comments on the nature of organizational change and a listing of test publishers and consultancies. There is also a glossary which provides definitions of key words and expressions – a useful resource in an area which has more than its fair share of jargon.

In summary, this book is about helping you to understand how psychology can be used to improve your business. The main sections deal with the most widely used and powerful techniques, and provide up-to-date information on:

- analysing and measuring jobs
- effective methods of selecting staff
- motivating and monitoring performance
- forming strong and productive teams
- focusing training and staff development
- stress control and workplace counselling
- finding and using business psychologists.

The idea is to introduce a range of tools that can be used in your organization, whatever its size. In this way *Using Psychology in Business* will appeal to all managers who want to get the best out of their people.

Measuring and Defining Jobs

Overview

The process of defining the qualities of a job, and of the person who is going to perform it, is of critical importance to every area of business psychology. It should also be of interest to all managers, whatever their department or function because, as is universally acknowledged, 'if you can't measure it, you can't manage it'. That is why it is the logical starting-point for job descriptions and person specifications, which are at the core of staff selection. Because it is a technique which can be used to identify the similarities in job content across levels of responsibility it forms the basis of reward management and is a prerequisite for designing effective training programmes. Finally, it can help in the audit of jobs and allow for 'benchmarking', or act in a strategic sense through the development of company-wide competency frameworks.

Defining jobs

Technically, the systematic study of job requirements is called 'job analysis' and is concerned with the content of a job or the behaviours required to do it. In this way, there are two distinct points of reference, and thus two main approaches, to job analysis. If the content is examined, the focus is on a comprehensive and exhaustive process of specification which concentrates on listing the precise work tasks that comprise a job. When properly performed, this sort of in-depth analysis covers every aspect of the job and can be used to draft work instructions – in other words, the detail is at a fine enough level to allow a manual of instructions to be produced. Indeed, a full specification in these terms can easily yield hundreds of instructions. However, such an approach does not produce a description of the knowledge, skills, abilities or experience required to do a job, although these can generally be inferred from the information that is gathered. In consequence, it can provide valuable information for formulating job descriptions, defining competencies, identifying performance indicators and so on.

The behavioural approach is concerned with specifying the particular 'behaviours' which are required to perform a job. These include such factors as knowledge, skills, experience, abilities, personality, values, attitudes and interests, and also cover the sort of areas which are used to develop a person specification, the latter being the information that is required, for example, to compose effective job advertisements or develop lists of targeted interview questions. However, although a link is made between the behaviours which are identified as being important to on-the-job performance, the approach is not as rigorous as that previously described.

Job analysis techniques

Whatever the focus of a job analysis there are six key techniques which are used to gather information. These are all widely used in the UK and other countries, and provide structured ways of defining the tasks and behaviours which comprise a job.

The techniques, which are often used in combination, are:

- job analysis interviews
- work profiling
- critical incidents
- focus groups
- repertory grids
- visionary interviews.

All six allow for the scientific analysis of jobs and consequently help to reduce the arbitrary way in which jobs are often defined. They also protect against many aspects of unfairness and prejudice, whether conscious or not, and so provide the groundwork for the elimination of many problems which arise through the infringement of employment laws, particularly those which relate to direct and indirect discrimination with regard to equal opportunities, sex, race and disability legislation.

Job analysis interviews

The job analysis interview is the simplest approach but it is also one of the easiest to carry out badly, since it relies on developing a set of structured questions which cover all the important aspects of a job, coupled with a style of interviewing that encourages job-holders to describe what they do fully and honestly. In the hands of a skilled interviewer this approach can provide detailed information on job activities and the sort of person needed to perform them. It also has the distinct advantage that it requires no specialist training (assuming a competent interview technique) and is quick and easy to use. The type of information that is uncovered lends itself to a process of straightforward analysis and can be used with data from any existing documentation. In addition, it can either be combined with material from job observations, which involve observing and classifying all the work activities performed by a job-holder, or with new job descriptions written by job-holders themselves. The latter can be based on self-reported material such as diaries, or logs which record the type, pattern and timing of activities over a typical working week.

If you wish to conduct your own job analysis interview you need to consider a number of things before you start. As part of your preparation you will require an outline description of the job and a detailed set of suitable questions – see the questionnaire on pp 4–7. You must also design a form on which to record the answers. This can, of course, just be a series of pages in a file, each keyed to a specific question, but you do need to do this in advance. Additionally, you will need to consider carefully who to interview. In most situations this will involve identifying at least two suitably skilled and experienced people who are able and willing to be interviewed. Finally, whoever is selected, it is important to prepare them so that they know what to expect. In particular, and to allay any anxiety, you will need to reassure your interviewees on a number of points – specifically that the interview is not an appraisal of their performance, a job evaluation (linked to pay), a 'test' or an assessment but that it is designed to discover what they perceive as their principal aims, duties and responsibilities. You should also emphasize that there are no 'right' or 'wrong' answers and that, while you may be making notes on what they say, all the information provided will be treated in the strictest confidence. Obviously, given the last point, this sort of interview needs to be conducted on an individual basis in a private location. This will probably mean talking to the interviewee, for at least an hour, in a place where you will not be disturbed.

Structured interview questionnaire

The following questionnaire covers the main parts of a job analysis. However, you should remember that not all the questions will be equally appropriate, and you will need to adapt some of them to the specific job you are examining. When required you will also need to indicate the importance of a particular activity and the length of time spent on it. This can be done quite easily by using three- (or five-) point scales. For example, you could rate activities as 'essential' (3), 'important' (2) or 'unimportant' (1), and break down time spent into 'most of the time' (3), 'some of the time' (2) and 'rarely' (1).

The questionnaire covers the context and aim of the job, principal duties, work activities, qualifications, experience, supervision and working relationships of the job-holder.

JOB ANALYSIS QUESTIONNAIRE*
Part A: Job context

1 What is the name (or title) of your present position?
2 Which department (or division) do you work in?
3 Who is your manager (or who do you report to)?
4 Who do you work with?
5 What is the name of the job above yours?
6 What is the name of the job below yours?

Tip: One way to discover the answers to questions 1–6 is to get the interviewee to sketch an organizational chart.

Part B: Aim of the job

7 What would you describe as the main aim (or objective) of your job?
8 Do you think there are any other, lesser aims, which are also important?

Part C: Principal duties

9 Describe your main work duties.
    9.1 Which are the most important?
    9.2 How much time do you spend on each of these?
    9.3 Which do you think are less important?
    9.4 How much time do you spend on each of these?

Tip: Go through the duties one at a time and explain your rating system. It is much easier if the interviewee decides if something is a '1', '2' or a '3'.

Part D: Work activities

10 What sort of written information (books, reports, manuals) do you use?
    10.1 What do you use written information for?
    10.2 Is it important for your work? (Rate 1–3.)
    10.3 Do you use written information often? (Rate 1–3.)
    10.4 What writing do you do as part of your job?
    10.5 How often do you write things? (Rate 1–3.)

Cont'd

*   This modified extract is taken from *Job Analysis: A Manager's Guide* by Michael Pearn and Rajvinder Kandola. It is reproduced by permission of the publishers, The Institute of Personnel and Development, IPD House, 35 Camp Road, London SW19 4UX.

11 What sort of numerical information (tables, balance sheets) do you use?
    11.1 What do you use numerical information for?
    11.2 Is it important for your work? (Rate 1–3.)
    11.3 Do you use numerical information often? (Rate 1–3.)
    11.4 What sort of calculations do you do as part of your job?
    11.5 How often do you have to calculate things? (Rate 1–3.)

12 What sort of visual information (graphs, charts, diagrams) do you use?
    12.1 What do you use visual information for?
    12.2 Is it important to your work? (Rate 1–3.)
    12.3 Do you use visual information often? (Rate 1–3.)
    12.4 What sort of visual information do you produce?
    12.5 How often do you produce visual information? (Rate 1–3.)

13 What sort of computer programs (spreadsheets, databases) do you use?
    13.1 What do you use computer programs for?
    13.2 Are they important for your work? (Rate 1–3.)
    13.2 Do you use computer programs often? (Rate 1–3.)
    13.3 What sort of computer-based information do you produce?
    13.4 How often do you produce such information? (Rate 1–3.)

14 Which parts of your job require accurate working?
    14.1 Why do you have to work accurately?
    14.2 How important is it to work accurately? (Rate 1–3.)
    14.3 How often do you work accurately? (Rate 1–3.)

Tip: For some jobs you will need to ask similar sets of questions about work tools or equipment, and also about any activities that require a significant physical effort – for example, lifting, pushing or carrying items of particular sizes or weights.

Part E: Qualifications

15 Do you require particular qualifications to do your job?
    15.1 What level of academic qualifications (none–degree) are required?
    15.2 Do you need any practical (craft or trade) qualifications? Which?
    15.3 Do you need professional (graduate or postgraduate) qualifications? Which?

Cont'd

Part F: Experience

16 Do you need previous experience to do your job?
    16.1 What sort of experience is required?
    16.2 How much experience do you need to be competent?
    16.3 What would happen if somebody wasn't experienced enough?

Tip: When asking about qualifications and experience it's important to isolate exactly why the job-holder feels that particular levels are important.

Part G: Supervision

17 Who supervises/manages your work?
    17.1 Is it important that your work is supervised/managed? (Rate 1–3.)
    17.1 How often is your work supervised/managed? (Rate 1–3.)
    17.2 How does the supervisor/manager know your work is up to standard?

18 Do you supervise/manage other people?
    18.1 How many people do you supervise/manage?
    18.2 How do you supervise/manage others?
    18.3 How important is it that you do this? (Rate 1–3.)
    18.4 How often are you involved in supervisory/management activities? (Rate 1–3.)

Tip: You may also wish to ask about other supervisory or management activities such as planning or scheduling, or things like quality and safety responsibilities. In addition, it can be useful to obtain information on the balance between routine and non-routine activities. Finally, for some jobs, you will need to determine whether the job-holder is personally responsible for money or other assets.

Part H: Working relationships

19 What sort of people do you deal with in the organization?
    19.1 Why do you need to have contact with these people?
    19.2 How important is it that you have contact with these people? (Rate 1–3.)
    19.3 How often do you have contact with these people? (Rate 1–3.)

Cont'd

20 Do you deal with people outside the organization?
    20.1 Who do you deal with?
    20.2 How do you deal with them (face-to-face, telephone, letter, fax, e-mail)?
    20.3 How important is it that you deal with them? (Rate 1–3.)
    20.4 How often do you deal with them? (Rate 1-3.)

Tip: For external relationships you may need to gather information on items like travel arrangements, distances and locations.

Additional information

To complete the picture it is usual to ask a series of questions about the work environment. These might include questions about working inside or outside, in an office or a factory, and under what conditions. Is it noisy, hot, cold, wet and so on?

The information you will obtain from a questionnaire of this nature is of a qualitative and quantitative nature. You will need to decide the relative importance of both types of information and integrate the data from all the people whom you interview. Generally, with regard to the quantitative element it is sufficient to average out the ratings to discover the relative importance of different activities.

Work profiling

While the structured interview provides a useful way of analysing most types of job, it is possible to purchase ready-made questionnaires and have them professionally analysed. These are often available in paper-and-pencil and computer-administered formats. Like the interview approach they break jobs down into tasks and activities and invite the interviewee to indicate the relevance of each, how often it is performed and so on. One advantage of this approach is that it is easy to combine the information from a large number of job-holders and, if desired, from their supervisors and managers as well. It is also possible to combine information from a number of different jobs. This means that a range of highly organized and structured information can be produced, which can be used as the starting-point for the specification of new jobs or positions – especially if data is gathered on future developments and activities. An example of the data provided by a computer-based system is presented in Table 1.1. This gives ratings for the 'intellectual' components of a job as provided by the job-holder and his or her manager. The 'future' column comprises the ratings given by the manager on the likely importance of

Table 1.1   'Intellectual' ratings

	Job-holder	Rating Boss	Future
Information collection	4.5	5	5
Problem analysis	4	4.5	5
Numerical interpretation	1.3	2	3.5
Judgement	4.5	4.5	4
Critical faculty	3.5	3.5	4.5
Creativity	2.5	3	4
Planning	3.5	2.5	4
Perspective	3.5	3	4
Organizational awareness	2.5	2.5	4
External awareness	2	2.5	3.5
Learning-oriented	2.5	3.5	3.5
Technical expertise	3	3	4

each component of the target job in three years' time. All the ratings are derived from a five-point scale, with the maximum being '5' ('vital').

The computer-analysed questionnaire generates a great deal of numerical information. However, there is potential for error and it is obviously very important that the correct data is entered in the first place. There are also issues concerning the costs of operating such systems, with some requiring information to be returned to the USA for analysis. Furthermore, the reports that are produced are often quite technical in nature and require skilled interpretation. This means that all users must be suitably trained.

The most popular computer-analysed questionnaire is the *Position Analysis Questionnaire* (PAQ®). This is published in the USA by the Purdue Research Foundation, and is available in the UK from Oxford Psychologists Press Ltd. It also comes in a managerial and professional form called the *Professional Managerial Position Questionnaire* (PMPQ®).

Other widely used products are the *Work Profiling System* (WPS), which is used on an international basis and published in the UK by Saville & Holdsworth Ltd; and the newer, *Job Analysis Questionnaire*, published in the UK by ASE.

Critical incidents

The critical incident technique is a type of interview designed to uncover examples of behaviour that have had a significant effect on work performance. It depends on identifying key incidents which demonstrate particularly 'effective' or 'ineffective' behaviour. When used in the correct context it represents a very flexible approach which can be conducted with job-holders and their immediate supervisors or manager. It can also be performed on an individual or group basis, although it should be recognized that there may be problems with getting people to admit to 'failure' in a group setting.

Technically, for an incident to be critical it must have taken place in a situation in which the outcome was noticeable and the consequences obvious. This means that the incident must be:

- clearly related to performance
- easily and accurately remembered
- capable of being classified.

The 'criticality' of an incident often depends on the perception of the person being interviewed. Thus, in many cases, interviewees – especially senior managers – will say that everything they do is critical. Nevertheless, if behaviours are analysed it is generally possible to determine the relative importance of actions, and thus to discover what combination of events led to success or failure. In a similar way some people claim that most of what they do is not critical and doesn't matter. Again, the best way to deal with this response is to explain that performance is affected by a range of behaviours which, when taken individually, may appear to be unimportant, but when combined do produce a significant result.

As you can see, there are some important prerequisites for the successful use of this approach. Nevertheless, most people find it an interesting experience and actually enjoy comparing and contrasting different aspects of their work performance; and there's no doubt that it can produce a view of work that is difficult to obtain in any other way.

In practice, when an incident has been identified and the context explained, you will need to ask a series of linked questions such as the following:

- When did it happen?
- Who was involved?
- What did you do?
- Why did you do it?
- What were the consequences?

- Why were these satisfactory/unsatisfactory?
- What did you learn?
- What actions would you take in the future?

To make use of this sort of anecdotal information it is necessary: to gather data on many incidents; for the interviewee to have actually experienced the incident; and, obviously, for it to be related to a specific job. Also, the technique relies on past behaviour and thus cannot be used to 'analyse' new positions.

The critical incident technique is suitable for analysing a wide range of activities. When used in a probing way it distinguishes at a practical level between 'good' and 'bad' job performance. However, there are a number of disadvantages, which include the fact that individuals must have clear memories of what happened, and that some events are more memorable than others – usually disasters! What about the times when everything went according to plan?

Criticisms aside, the approach is easy to apply and requires little training, although it is advisable for the administrators to have well developed interview skills. It should also be remembered that a large number of interviews will have to be conducted in order to get a good idea of the critical behaviours in a particular job. This can be quite hard work as some people take to the technique quite readily, while others find it difficult to describe enough incidents – as a rule of thumb, you should expect to get information on about six incidents from each person interviewed. Finally, it is wise not to depend solely on this technique, but to amalgamate the information with some of the other approaches described.

Focus groups

The focus group is an organized discussion forum. It is applicable to all levels of staff and is generally used to clarify the purpose, behaviours and actions required to perform particular job activities. This means that it requires a list of predefined questions, or information from other job analysis techniques, which participants can discuss. The group format also means that it requires careful supervision, which implies the involvement of one or two trained facilitators who should make sure that each question is addressed, that everyone has a chance to talk, and that the results of the discussion are accurately recorded.

In order for a focus group to generate useful information it is necessary for the following conditions to be met:

- The discussion must have a precise focus.
- Sufficient time must be allowed.

■ The discussion must be led.
■ Information must be recorded as the discussion progresses.

The latter might involve using whiteboards, flipcharts, Post-it notes or anything which allows the information to be captured as it is produced. Facilitators should also be prepared for lengthy sessions as most focus groups take two or three hours, but the fact that focus groups run over long time periods and involve a number of people helps the process of gathering a representative sample of behaviour. The dynamics of a group situation also allow people to build on each other's ideas and to explore new aspects of a job.

The drawbacks relate to getting people to talk or, sometimes, getting people to stop talking! Also some participants feel threatened or inhibited by other group members, especially if their immediate manager is present. There's also a danger of discussions becoming 'complaining' sessions in which people only describe what is wrong with a particular job. All these potential problems can be resolved, but they do rely on the skills of the facilitators. In particular, facilitators need to be experienced in the use of verbal and non-verbal communication methods. For example, contributions need to be acknowledged with a 'yes' and a smile or a nod. It's also important to maintain eye contact with the person talking and to angle the body towards them, to ask open-ended questions and to be able to summarize and reflect on what is being said. This requires a good deal of energy, well developed listening skills and, last but not least, the ability to deal with periods of silence.

Like all the techniques described so far it is possible to organize discussion groups without special training. However, if you are not an experienced facilitator it can be difficult to run one effectively without any practice. For instance, newcomers find it especially difficult to manage the information from a number of contributors while simultaneously making detailed notes.

Repertory grid

It is beyond the scope of this book to give a full description of the repertory grid – or, as it is more correctly known, the 'role construct repertory grid' – because it is a complex psychological technique which requires considerable training and practice to use effectively. Consequently, if you wish to have a job analysis performed using this technique you should seek the services of a business psychologist or attend a professional training course. However, the gist of the approach is that we understand the world, and the people in it, by attaching particular meanings to our experiences.

The meanings which we attach to events form the basis on which we assess other events and the way in which we filter new information.

So, in some respects, we all act like scientists searching for meanings (or explanations), developing personal theories, putting things to the test, and revising our view of the world in light of what we discover. Technically, this is known as construing the world in order to develop a construct system.

The constructs that we use frame the way in which we look at other people. They also allow us to predict what another person is likely to do. In this way we are implicitly assuming that constructs are dimensional, in that they have two ends. In other words, if we can predict that something is likely to happen, it follows that we have some way of predicting how unlikely it is to happen. In turn this process rests on us being able to recognize the similarities and differences between things in a way which makes sense to us as individuals. In grid terms what we are talking about are bipolar constructs – for example, 'experienced–inexperienced', 'cooperative–confrontational', 'logical–intuitive' and so on. These are the filters through which we progressively assess new information.

The repertory grid is a technique for revealing the construct systems relating to a particular topic, such as the relationship between sets of work activities, or the variations in performance between different people. Once this focus has been decided on, the process relies on the identification of a suitable range of elements (the work activities or people in question) and the constructs which relate to them. The analysis then concentrates on the way in which each element is assessed on each construct. This usually involves selecting three elements at random and asking the participant in what way two of the elements are alike, and how they differ from the third. This produces the two poles of the construct and, once this has been done for every combination, all the elements are rated against each construct. An example grid for a telemarketing job is reproduced in Figure 1.1.

When the process is completed the information is analysed by computer. This provides a picture of each participant's view of their job and can also be used to compare one person's view with that of another. In some ways, the information gathered is similar to that obtained by the critical incident technique, but this process is far more exhaustive. It is particularly effective at uncovering aspects of job performance that are not, strictly speaking, observable – for example, core values, decision-making style and underlying managerial approach.

The disadvantages are that it cannot be conducted as a group session, thereby making it very time-consuming, and sometimes only vague information is gathered if interviewers are not properly trained.

Visionary interviews

This final technique is important for understanding the requirements of new or future jobs. It relies on interviewing a suitable cross-section of

Activities (elements) \ Skills (constructs)	Negotiation skill	Persuasive ability	Initiative	Oral communication	Detail consciousness	Information-gathering	Tenacity	Stress tolerance	Decisiveness	Customer orientation
Identifying target groups	1	1	5	1	5	5	3	1	3	5
Compiling 'prospect' lists	1	1	5	2	5	5	3	1	1	5
Establishing customer needs	1	1	4	4	5	5	3	1	3	5
Setting call objectives	1	2	3	2	5	3	3	1	4	3
Making cold calls	5	5	5	5	4	3	4	4	5	5
Dealing with difficult customers	5	5	3	5	4	4	4	5	5	5
Closing sales	5	5	3	5	4	3	5	3	5	3
Arranging for payment	3	4	3	4	5	4	2	1	5	3
Organizing despatch of goods	2	2	2	2	4	4	1	1	1	3
Monitoring performance	1	1	3	2	4	5	1	2	2	2

Fig 1.1 Telemarketing repertory grid

Note: The ratings range from '1' (unimportant) to '5' (essential).

'visionaries', or those with a view of the organization's future. This is important because the preceding techniques are mostly concerned with gathering information from existing job-holders about their current jobs. What is needed to complete the picture is information on the future needs of the organization in terms of changes to objectives, values, and work behaviour. Such interviews also ensure that the future commercial environment is taken into account, along with any changes to the organization's 'culture'. The latter may include moves to flatter management structures, with a greater emphasis on more open communication, individual decision-making, results orientation and so on.

When conducting visionary interviews it is often better to adopt an open-ended format and not to impose a particular structure on the proceedings. However, that is not to say that you should not have a list of opening questions, or that critical incident or repertory grid techniques cannot be used. Rather, the issue is one of sensitivity of approach, especially when dealing with senior executives. Therefore adapt your approach to take into account the personal 'style' of the interviewee and concentrate on establishing the medium- to long-term goals of the organization. Once the goals have been clarified ask about the sorts of behaviour which will be required to meet them.

Critically, the sorts of question which you need to explore are those which concern the main areas of organizational change. These are:

- **Strategic**. Are there likely to be any strategic shifts in work activity? New products or services? New markets? Are there plans to operate in other countries? To merge activities? Form joint ventures? Expand into completely new business areas?
- **Technological**. What changes are likely to production or process activities? Will technology change the way in which services are delivered? How might technology influence functions such as research and development, finance, marketing or human resource management?
- **Structural**. What changes will there be to the organizational structure? Will different forms of management be needed? How will responsibilities be assigned? How will information flow around the organization? How will individual roles be defined? How will relationships change?
- **People-oriented**. What new tasks will individuals be required to do? What implications will there be for training and career management? What new forms of group or team work will be required? How will teams (possibly operating in different parts of the world) interact with each other? How will performance be assessed?

All these 'variables' interact with each other: for example, strategic changes often have profound effects on organizational structure; as does technology on what people actually do. The key is to try to predict the most likely changes and thus to identify the new skills, abilities and working relationships that will be required in the future.

In practice the visionary interview and other techniques are combined to form a comprehensive job analysis. This can be a complex piece of work and a complete organizational analysis will take some time to complete – not least because the more information that is generated, the more complicated is the process of integrating the component parts. Also, consideration needs to be given to the 'weight' which will be given to each piece of information, as some information will be of a qualitative rather than a quantitative nature, and, of course, some activities will be more important than others. In many situations organizations are well advised to seek the assistance of a business psychologist to help them with this final stage. An example of a job analysis is given in the case study which follows.

Case Study: Job analysis in a bank

A major bank with over 80 000 employees decided to streamline its management structure. As part of the restructuring, all junior and middle management positions were subject to job analysis, and a number of new positions were created. The new positions were all concerned with the use of the latest computer-based financial management systems.

The process involved 100 managers who each completed a detailed job analysis questionnaire. In addition, a further 24 managers, six from each of the main divisions, provided critical incident information. These managers were selected, on the basis of ratings from their annual appraisal, as being representative of 'average' and 'superior' performers, the idea being that they would provide examples of both 'good' and 'bad' practice.

The data from the questionnaires and critical incidents was analysed and presented to a series of four focus groups composed of six managers from each division. They had the task of assessing their own job specifications for accuracy and completeness and were also asked to consider what factors would be important in the new positions under consideration. For example, what sort of IT skills would be required? Was previous banking experience strictly necessary? Were other sorts of experience more appropriate?

In parallel with the focus groups a cross-section of six senior executives took part in visionary interviews. They also completed a number of repertory grids. The interviews and the grids allowed a number of strategic factors to be isolated. These included: a need for managers who were capable of dealing with a more flexible working environment; a greater emphasis on 'transparent' communication within and between levels of management; greater scope for personal decision-making; and a more dynamic approach to management development, this being a key point as the bank wished to become recognized as a 'learning organization'.

The complete job analysis provided a blueprint for junior and middle management positions, allowing the reassessment of existing staff and the production of new job descriptions. The information generated also helped in the design of a new management development programme.

Multi-role working

One aspect of job analysis that is often overlooked is how to define multi-role work environments. These are workplaces in which people perform distinctly different work activities, each with their own performance criteria, which themselves change depending on the nature of the work being performed. For example, in many health care situations there is a tension between managerial and professional roles. In such situations there can be a genuine conflict between control and cost issues and those of primary patient care. Not surprisingly, this often means that individuals find it difficult to decide on an appropriate form of working behaviour that satisfies both sets of demands equally.

Similar issues arise in all multi-role jobs. Thus, any professional, whether they be an engineer, doctor, lawyer, teacher or similar, who also has 'staff' responsibilities, faces similar problems. Clearly, some way is required of identifying the boundaries of the different roles involved in a job and of highlighting the differences between individual, shared and peripheral work. It is really a question of prioritizing the different tasks a person has to complete against the overall objectives of a particular role, and a useful way of doing this is to take job analysis information and to order activities according to the following five categories:

- **Fixed.** These are activities which must be performed to a given standard – for example, delivering a service in line with a written quality standard.
- **Goal.** These are individual activities which are linked to a given objective – for example, increasing consultancy fee income by 25 per cent over a 12-month period.
- **Reactive.** These are activities which change according to work demands – for example, a manager serving in a restaurant at times of peak demand.
- **Shared.** These are activities for which a group or team has overall responsibility – for example, most management teams have shared responsibilities.
- **Creative.** These are new or serendipitous activities which lead to better ways of doing things – for example, a technician realizes that a process could be made more efficient by changing the sequence of activities.

These categories help tease out the differences between individual, shared and reactive activities. They also draw attention to those aspects of jobs which are flexible, which would include goal-driven activities because the method is often less important than the goal itself, and reactive tasks because they are, by definition, unpredictable. Likewise, shared tasks are usually flexible as well.

Once work activities have been classified in this way, job specifications can reflect the balance between fixed activities and those which are changeable. This helps add a dynamic element to specifications and allows for a degree of individual variation. After all, different people can perform the same job in different ways as long as they fulfil all their roles appropriately.

Example: person specification

In a full specification each of the attributes listed would be expanded and described in terms of the relevant behavioural indicators. As mentioned, a distinction would also be made, for example, between fixed and shared activities. In addition, an indication would be given of future job requirements – for instance, in this case, a knowledge of doing business through the internet might be appropriate.

Job title:	Sales Administration Manager	**Job grade:**	10
Location:	Head Office	**Reporting:**	Sales Director

Knowledge: Main products and services (E)
EU export controls (E)
Commercial legislation (E)
Key competitors (D)
UK economic indicators (D)

Skills/abilities: Teambuilding (E)
Conflict management (E)
Financial forecasting (E)
Risk management (E)
Verbal communication (E)
Numerical and statistical analysis (E)
$2 \times$ European languages (D)

Experience: Sales administration (E – 2 years+)
Profit & loss accounting (E – 2 years+)
Managing sales teams (E – 3 years+)

Industry sector (E – 5 years+)
Key account management (D)
Progression management (D)

Competencies*:   Resilient (E)
Persevering (E)
Team-minded (E)
Flexible (E)
Business-oriented (E)
Concern for excellence (E)
Innovative (D)
Personal impact (D)

Note: 'E' means that an attribute is essential, 'D' that it is desirable.
* See 'Competency frameworks', pp 18–21.

Competency frameworks

A thorough job analysis produces the raw material for job specifications. As such, it helps to define the knowledge, skills and abilities (KSAs) and, in turn, other factors, such as personality characteristics, which are related to competent performance. In many situations this is all that is required, and a list of KSAs is a perfectly adequate starting-point for a person specification. However, a more sophisticated way of using job analysis information is to develop a list of job 'competencies' – a method of defining job requirements that has already been alluded to in the descriptions used for job analysis questionnaires (Table 1.1) and repertory grids (Figure 1.1).

A competency is a cluster of personal characteristics which influence how a job is performed. It is focused on what people actually do, or those aspects of their behaviour which can be directly observed, and in particular those factors which lead to superior job performance. Consequently, most competencies comprise a number of underlying KSAs. Furthermore, when all the key competencies have been identified for a given job (or jobs) they can provide a complete 'framework' against which to assess other people. However, before we consider competencies in greater detail it is important to highlight the differences between 'competencies' and 'competences'. As mentioned, competencies relate to the person and are concerned with the context of different sorts of behaviour, whereas competences are concerned with the job itself and centre on the complexity of a task or its output. Thus a 'communication' *competency* might involve conveying information in a clear, accurate and convincing way; on the other hand communication *competence* might involve being able to write grammatically correct sentences free from spelling errors. Obviously, the two will overlap on occasions but competences are usually only concerned with specific tasks.

An important aspect of competency frameworks is that they provide evidence of performance. Thus competencies not only summarize specific aspects of behaviour, but are expressed in terms of behavioural 'performance' indicators. These tell the observer what to look for in terms of 'above' and 'below' average performance, or depending on the application, the competencies which should be exhibited at different levels in an organization. An example of a typical competency is given in Table 1.2. As you can see from the table, there are a number of positive performance indicators. However, the list could easily have covered a range of negative indicators such as:

- bases decisions on incomplete information
- makes decisions on an intuitive basis
- does not accept responsibility for decisions
- avoids making difficult decisions, and so on.

Table 1.2   Decision-making competency

Competency: decision-making

Definition

Decision-making competency is the ability to identify sources of relevant and objective information, analyse them in a systematic way, draw logical conclusions and then to make decisions with due regard to time constraints and business priorities.

Performance indicators

Identifies relevant information	Makes decisions within time allowed
Evaluates available information	Can make unpopular decisions if required
Challenges assumptions	Can make decisions in absence of precedence
Draws logical conclusions	Assesses costs and benefits of decisions
Establishes and prioritizes tasks	Takes personal responsibility for decisions

Another refinement is to group the indicators in terms of level of performance or experience. Thus we could develop a system of five gradings, with Level 1 indicating 'low' or 'inexperienced' performance and Level 5 'expert' or 'highly skilled' performance. The middle grading, Level 3, would indicate 'average' or 'proven' performance. A grading system for the decision-making competency is presented in Table 1.3.

Table 1.3   Competency level indicators

Level 1 (no experience)

- Decision-making is erratic and unstructured
- Important information is missed
- No real prioritization
- Need for ongoing supervision

Level 2 (basic experience)

- Decision-making is based on the identification of key issues
- All easily accessed information is assessed
- Experience is used to make discriminatory judgements
- Acceptable results are produced

Level 3 (proven ability)

- Decision-making takes into account general business issues
- A broad range of material is analysed
- Conflicting information is assessed
- A number of options are considered

Level 4 (extensive experience)

- Sound reasoning is applied to all decisions
- Decision-making is based on a wide range of business factors
- Personal responsiblity is taken for difficult decisions
- Ability to act decisively in crisis situations.

Level 5 (expert)

- Decision-making automatically covers all relevant sources of information
- Confident, effective and timely decisions are always made
- Advises others on decision-making strategies
- Decisions take into account strategic business position

An important thing to realize about grading systems is that they provide a more accurate way of assessing individuals against job requirements This is of particular value in selection and appraisal situations, and also provides a method of differentiating between different levels in an organization.

How many competencies?

The competency method is popular because it provides a common language for business development. It is also an efficient way of specifying jobs because most can be covered by 10 or 12 individual competencies. However, there is no magic number and the Royal Mail, the UK's principal letter delivery service, has, for example, ten core competencies, as does Tarmac, the international construction group; on the other hand, Xerox, the office technology company, has a management model which contains 32! The Xerox approach, which is often referred to as the '23+9', incorporates 23 leadership competencies such as 'strategic thinking' and 'decision-making', and nine cultural dimensions including such elements as 'team oriented' and 'line-driven'. The company believes that if managers embody all the competencies then it will meet its target of becoming a $10 billion-turnover company by the year 2005. This is an example of competencies driving a powerful strategic vision.

In some ways, the number of competencies used in a particular framework is unimportant. However, the number must be manageable, and all have to be directly related to the job or jobs in question. It is also possible to identify a number of additional requirements. Competencies need to be:

- **Comprehensive**. The list of competencies must give complete coverage of all the important work activities. As mentioned this can usually be achieved with 10–12 core competencies.
- **Discrete**. An individual competency must relate to a definable activity which can be clearly differentiated from other activities. If competencies overlap it is difficult to assess people or jobs with precision.
- **Focused**. Each competency must be tightly defined and must not attempt to cover too much ground – this is sometimes referred to as 'chunk size'. For example, a 'technical' competency may need to be extremely specific.
- **Accessible**. Each competency must be expressed in an understandable way so that they can be used universally. There is no point in using excessive corporate jargon as this may not be understood in the same way by all managers.
- **Congruent**. The competencies must reinforce the organization's culture and long-term aims. If the competencies seem too abstract they will not be useful and managers will not 'buy in' to the approach.

■ **Up-to-date.** A competency system must be kept up-to-date and should reflect the present and (predictable) future needs of an organization. As with any job analysis technique this requires input from those with strategic vision.

Developing a competency framework

As demonstrated by Table 1.2 a competency has three parts. These are a title, a definition and a list of performance indicators. In addition, in circumstances where it is important to measure level of performance the indicators will be grouped according to a rating scale.

To develop a framework it is necessary to collect a large sample of job analysis data and to sort it into competency clusters, using, for example some of the following labels: 'intellectual', 'personal', 'interpersonal', 'communication', 'leadership' and 'results-oriented'. This task is better carried out by a group, rather than an individual, as the end result will be more objective. Once consensus has been reached on the clusters the group should compose suitable definitions for all the component competencies. The next stage is to isolate performance indicators and to rank them by level. When a rough draft of the complete framework has been achieved each competency should be double-checked for usability, fairness and relevance. Finally, it is useful to ask the following questions:

■ Does each competency focus on a well defined group of behaviours?
■ Can the behaviours described be easily observed and 'measured'?
■ Are behaviours expressed in terms of what people do (actions)?
■ Is the context in which the behaviours are expected made explicit?
■ Are behaviours equally applicable to men, women and other groups?
■ Is the language used fair, unbiased and free of unnecessary jargon?
■ Do the competencies cover all aspects of the job in question?
■ Has provision been made for the technical aspects of particular jobs?
■ Do the competencies fully encompass the context of the business?
■ Do the competencies take into account likely future developments?

The two most common mistakes when drafting competencies are to make them too vague or to inadvertently exclude certain groups. For example, many competency frameworks have an 'interpersonal' component. But this is a very broad term and includes a wide range of behaviours such as influencing, persuading, asserting, empathizing, supporting, helping, caring, encouraging, socializing, cooperating, encouraging and listening; not to mention appraising, coaching, developing, confronting, and every other conceivable aspect of selling, managing and teamwork. Obviously, a degree of clarity is vital if the framework is to be a workable proposition. Likewise, great care should be taken when defining strategic competencies such as those concerned with leadership because different leadership approaches have been shown to be influenced by factors such as gender – a problem which can be compounded if competencies are defined by all-male groups which may undervalue approaches which are more typical of women. This might lead to giving unnecessary weight to 'transactional' styles (those that involve giving direction and exercising formal authority) over more 'transformational' styles, in which the concern is with motivating and empowering others to achieve organizational goals.

Finally, it is always possible to obtain help with defining competencies, either by retaining the services of a consultant or by using a suitable reference source. Thus you can get inspiration from listings of competencies or competency dictionaries which can provide a useful starting-point for your own framework and reduce the tendency to 'reinvent the wheel'. An example listing from the Job Analysis Questionnaire (JAQ) is given at the end of this chapter (pp 25–28).

Benchmarking

An important way of refining competency models is to incorporate benchmarking information. In essence, this requires an organization to measure aspects of its own performance against other organizations recognized as expert in a particular area. For example, a company interested in improving its distribution network could benchmark itself against an expert logistics operation, or an organization which sells products or services over the telephone could assess its performance against a leading telemarketing company. Whatever the comparison – and it is important that it is against an organization which is recognized as operating at an expert level in a particular sector – there are a number of key stages to the benchmarking process.

First, areas which are amenable to improvement must be selected. This means picking competencies carefully and developing performance indicators which allow meaningful comparisons to be made. Clearly, if benchmarking is to work there is no point in producing a set of indicators that only have meaning to your own organization. Second, choose appropriate organizations from which to obtain information. These may be leaders in your own business sector or 'champions' from other areas. Next, study the data rigorously and identify opportunities for improvement. This should provide focused performance data which you can incorporate in your own competency framework. Finally, implement the revised competencies.

The most difficult part of the process is obtaining information from other organizations. However, it is possible to gather useful data from 'public' sources. These include, in the UK at least, the performance indicators set by bodies such as the Audit Commission; national surveys, and databases maintained by professional organizations and consultancy groups. You can also circulate questionnaires to target organizations or obtain information from benchmarking 'clubs'. These are informal groupings of organizations which pool performance information. For example, there is a UK based Financial Services Special Interests Group and also international consultancies, such as Hay/McBer, that promote benchmarking excellence.

While benchmarking may be a useful mechanism for improving competencies it does entail a number of problems. One is the use of 'input' information to indicate the quality of 'outputs'. For example, you may have a customer service competency which involves responding to customer enquiries as quickly as possible. However, despite the fact that a quick response is usually desirable, this would give no indication of quality of service. Indeed, operators rated as giving quick service may not be dealing with the customers' real needs. Other problems involve the collection of performance data that is considered commercially sensitive. Clearly, there is no way of making firms reveal such information, but issues like these do point towards considering sources such as benchmarking clubs.

In summary, benchmarking is one of the most effective ways of identifying opportunities for improvement and tuning a competency model because it allows organizations to focus on areas in which action can produce the greatest rewards.

Using job analysis techniques

It is impossible to overemphasize the importance of effective job analysis. It may not appear to be a particularly exciting activity but it is the cornerstone of all successful interventions. Unless a manager knows what competencies a job demands, and how these are likely to evolve over time, it is impossible to produce an effective selection and assessment process – or, for that matter, any focused development activity.

Unfortunately, job descriptions and person specifications are often produced using a seat-of-the-pants method which falls far short of being either objective or systematic. Such unscientific approaches do no service to either potential employees or employer organizations. Job analysis must involve one or all of the techniques described in this chapter, and, at the very least, a structured questionnaire should be used. Critical incident, focus group and visionary interviews can also add important information. Other techniques, such as the repertory grid, require specialist training and experience and are usually performed by business psychologists. It is also the case that some work profiling questionnaires are only available through psychologists or require managers to attend public training courses.

The widespread use of competency frameworks has led to many freely available resources. However, the development of a framework from scratch – particularly if it has to cover multi-role working – is a complex and time-consuming process. For this reason, many organizations use the services of a consultant. This can actually save money as most consultants have a detailed understanding of generic competencies, performance indicators and so forth, and can concentrate on tailoring frameworks to the specific requirements of the client organization. The same argument applies to benchmarking, as it is only very large organizations that usually have the luxury of participating in benchmarking clubs. A knowledgeable consultant will save much time and effort and will often be familiar with best practice in a range of different organizations.

Job analysis checklist

- Always select a fully representative sample of job-holders.
- Involve managers at all levels in the organization.
- Use a number of complementary job analysis techniques.
- Make sure that future job requirements are addressed.
- Check that specifications are fair and unbiased.
- Ensure that job requirements are described in action terms.
- Use clear and easily understood definitions.
- Allow for flexible work roles and conditions.
- Link specifications, or competencies, to business objectives.
- Aim to benchmark against recognized 'champions'.

Example JAQ Competency Definitions*

Intellectual
1 *Information Collection*
   Seeks all possible relevant information for tasks systematically. Elicits relevant information from others.
2 *Problem Analysis*
   Identifies a problem and breaks it down into its constituent parts. Links together and evaluates information from different sources, and identifies possible causes of problem.
3 *Numerical Interpretation*
   Assimilates numerical and statistical information accurately and makes sensible, sound interpretations.
4 *Judgement*
   Makes sensible, sound decisions or proposals based on reasonable assumptions and factual information.

5 *Critical Faculty*
Challenges existing facts and assumptions. Rapidly identifies the short-comings and flaws in a plan or proposal, and the reasons why it might not work.

6 *Creativity*
Produces highly imaginative and innovative ideas and proposals which are not obvious to less perceptive colleagues.

7 *Planning*
Establishes future priorities and visualises all foreseeable changes required to meet future requirements. Identifies appropriate resource requirements, including staff, to achieve long-term objectives.

8 *Perspective*
Rises above the immediate problem or situation and sees the broader issues and wider implications, relates facts and problems to an extremely wide context through an ability to perceive all possible relationships.

9 *Organizational Awareness*
Has extensive knowledge of organizational issues and is able to identify problems, threats and opportunities within the organization. Perceives the effect and the implications of own decisions on other parts of the organization.

10 *External Awareness*
Has extensive knowledge of issues and changes within external environment and is able to identify existing or potential strengths, weaknesses, opportunities and threats to the organization. Understands the effects and implications of external factors on own decisions.

11 *Learning-Orientated*
Actively identifies own learning needs and opportunities. Is effective in applying new learning in a work context.

12 *Technical Expertise*
Keeps relevant technical knowledge, skills and expertise up-to-date and applies them effectively.

Personal

13 *Adaptability*
Whenever placed in a new situation or culture, adapts behaviour rapidly to the new requirements and maintains effectiveness.

14 *Independence*
Behaviour is determined by own judgements, opinions and beliefs, and not unduly by those of other people.

15 *Integrity*
Is truthful, honest and trustworthy, and conforms to current ethical standards. Does not compromise on matters of principle.

16 *Stress Tolerance*
Whenever challenged or put under significant pressure, maintains performance level and does not appear to become irritable or anxious, or to lose composure.

17 *Resilience*
Maintains performance in the face of adversity. Does not react negatively to disappointments, insults or unfair remarks.

18 *Detail Consciousness*
Works precisely and accurately with highly detailed factual information. Is methodical and ensures detail is not overlooked.

19 *Self-Management*
Makes effective use of own time and other resources. Organizes paperwork efficiently and tidily, adopts effective filing and retrieval procedures.

20 *Change-Orientated*
Actively seeks to change the job and environment whenever appropriate. Is proactive, encourages the introduction of new structures, methods and procedures.

Communication

21 *Reading*
Shows by the use made of written information that it has been effectively assimilated and retained.

22 *Written Communication*
Written work is readily intelligible; points and ideas are conveyed clearly and concisely to the reader.

23 *Listening*
Listens dispassionately, is not selective in what has been heard; conveys the clear impression that key points have been recalled and taken into account.

24 *Oral Expression*
Is fluent, speaks clearly and audibly, and has good diction.

25 *Oral Presentation*
In formal presentations, is concise and to the point; does not use jargon without explanation; tailors content to the audience's understanding. Is enthusiastic and lively when speaking.

Inter-Personal

26 *Impact*
Makes a strong, positive impression on first meeting. Has authority and credibility; establishes rapport quickly with colleagues and customers.

27 *Persuasiveness*
Influences and persuades others to give their agreement and commitment to decision or course of action which they initially opposed.

28 *Sensitivity*
Is aware of the needs and feelings of staff, colleagues and customers, and responds accordingly.

29 *Flexibility*
Adopts a flexible but not compliant style when interacting with others. Takes their views into account and changes position when appropriate.

30 *Ascendancy*
Is forceful and assertive when dealing with others. Takes charge of a situation and commands the respect of others.

31 *Negotiating*
When negotiating, communicates proposals effectively, identifies a basis for compromise and reaches agreement with others through personal power and influence.

Leadership

32 *Organizing*
Sets tasks for subordinates and others to achieve current objectives, and co-ordinates their activities effectively. Organizes all resources efficiently and effectively.

33 *Empowering*
Distinguishes effectively between what should be done by others and what one should do oneself. Empowers subordinates by delegating all appropriate tasks and other responsibilities to them.

34 *Appraising*
Effectively monitors and evaluates the results of subordinates' work and provides feedback and advice whenever appropriate.

35 *Motivating Others*
Inspires others to achieve goals by showing vision and a clear idea of what needs to be achieved, and by showing commitment and enthusiasm.

36 *Developing Others*
Makes every effort to develop, both on and off the job, the knowledge, skills and competencies of subordinates, or others, required to advance their careers.

37 *Leading*
Gives clear direction and leads from the front whenever necessary. Fosters effective teamwork by involving subordinates and adopting the appropriate leadership style to achieve the team's goals.

Results-Orientation

38 *Risk Taking*
Makes decisions which involve a significant risk in order to achieve a recognized benefit or advantage. Seeks new experiences and situations rather than the security afforded by well-established or familiar ones.

39 *Decisiveness*
Prepared to make decisions or recommendations, or to show commitment, even if information is incomplete or of uncertain validity.

40 *Business Sense*
Identifies those opportunities which will increase the organization's sales or profits; selects and exploits those activities which will result in the largest returns.

41 *Energy*
Shows energy and vitality. Produces a high level of output. Works rapidly at all times so that a backlog does not build up.

42 *Concern for Excellence*
Sets stretching goals, and expects high standards of performance and quality from self and others. Continuously endeavours to improve standards and will not accept poor performance.

43 *Tenacity*
Shows an unwavering determination to achieve objectives when faced with setbacks or obstacles.

44 *Initiative*
Initiates action and influences events through own efforts. Is always seeking, and is keen to accept, additional tasks or responsibilities.

45 *Customer-Orientated*
Actively seeks to understand customers' requirements. Actions anticipate and pre-empt requests for service based on well-developed relationships.

Further information

Codling, S. (1995), *Best Practice Benchmarking*, Aldershot: Gower.

Hay Group (1996), *People and Competencies: The Route to Competitive Advantage*, London: Kogan Page.

Industrial Society (1996), *Managing Best Practice Series: Management Competencies*, London: Industrial Society.

Pearn, M. and Kandola, R. (1995), *Job Analysis: A Manager's Guide*, London: Institute of Personnel and Development.

Recruitment and Selection

Overview

This chapter explores some of the assessment techniques available to the business psychologist or manager with human resource (HR) responsibilities. All are designed to gather objective information about candidates and make the selection process fairer and more efficient. However, it must be emphasized that the starting-point for all these methods is a well structured job analysis and a detailed person specification. This provides a sound basis for the production of recruitment advertisements and literature, and generates the information required to produce effective application or biodata forms. Needless to say, a behavioural person specification is also of prime importance to the most commonly used selection device of them all – the interview. In fact, the 'traditional' biographical interview is used in over 90 per cent of selection situations; with its more sophisticated cousins, behavioural and situational interviews, used at the rates of 35 and 15 per cent respectively. In the following pages a number of ways of assessing candidates are examined, with particular attention being given to the sort of information they yield and to best practice.

Recruitment methods

In an employment context, the term 'recruitment' refers to the process of attracting job candidates. As such, it is concerned with the provision of job-related information by the employer and is essentially a selling process. In contrast 'selection' is about obtaining objective information from candidates and deciding whether they fit specific job criteria. This process often involves using a number of assessment methods such as application forms, psychometric tests and interviews. Nevertheless, there are times when selection and recruitment activities interact. For example, the interview may be considered to have a public relations role, as it gives the candidate an opportunity to 'assess' the organization. Similarly, the job advertisement allows for a degree of self-selection because potential candidates may select themselves 'in' or 'out' of the process on the basis of the information provided.

There are many different ways of attracting candidates. One informal method, 'word of mouth', is said by experts to account for up to 50 per cent of candidates. However, this recruitment method severely restricts the pool of candidates and may also infringe equal opportunities legislation, and employers should think carefully before giving preference to those found through casual contact, or incidentally through venues such as trade fairs and conferences, or even as a spin-off of direct mail. At the other extreme, there are numerous formal methods covering printed and electronic media, various types of employment agency and organizational activities. An indication of the range of methods is given below:

- **Print media:** newspapers, trade journals, professional journals, magazines.
- **Electronic media:** local radio, teletext, television, Internet.
- **External agencies:** employment agencies, job centres, recruitment consultants.
- **Organizational:** newsletters, noticeboards, open days, intranet.

Looking at these in more detail, the 'traditional' methods include the print media, such as local and national newspapers, trade or professional journals, as well as public and private employment agencies and specialist search organizations, such as 'headhunting' companies. Other techniques, which may be less familiar, are the use of the Internet and the advertising opportunities on the World-WideWeb (WWW), and the corporate intranet which is the electronic equivalent of the organizational noticeboard. In fact web-based recruitment activities are rapidly increasing in popularity, especially with regard to filling IT, technological and scientific vacancies. As ever, the USA is leading the way with as many as 35 000 recruitment sites in operation, and it is estimated that these are visited by 100 million job-hunters per year.

Whatever the chosen media, employers need to be conscious of the effect that advertisements have on the candidate pool. For example, a vague yet attractively worded advertisement may attract thousands of applications and is therefore not an efficient way of finding staff unless there are many jobs on offer. The aim should be to provide sufficient information for candidates to operate some degree of self-selection, otherwise the quantity of applications received will swamp the assessment process. In general, well constructed advertisements take advantage of factors like corporate image (a 'big' name), but temper this by providing accurate and detailed job information. Indeed, research has shown that job-hunters want as much basic information as possible and are actually put off by incomplete details. In short, there is nothing wrong with an attractive advertisement which presents an organization in a strong and positive light, but it must be balanced with some hard facts.

When external agencies are used, make sure that they can assess candidates against realistic and accurate criteria. Again, this depends on a thorough understanding of your requirements coupled with extensive and detailed job information. As recruitment consultancies can charge anywhere between 10–30 per cent of the first year's salary for filling a position, it is extremely important that you, the employer, provide the appropriate sort of job analysis information or that an analysis is performed on your behalf.

If you are in doubt about what sort of information to use in an advertisement, or are unsure about any of the legal aspects of recruitment, make sure that you consult a professional. This will probably save you money and will undoubtedly save you a great deal of time. In particular, you need to be wary of indirectly discriminating against particular candidates. For example, there was a classic case in the UK concerning an advertisement placed by the Civil Service Commission (who might have been expected to have access to expert opinion) which included an age range. This was held to be discriminatory because fewer women in the workforce were between the ages quoted, and so women as a group were likely to be subject to unfair discrimination. Similar situations can easily arise with regard to other sorts of employment legislation, such as those concerning race and disability. In other countries there are also provisions for members of different religious communities, and for factors like educational requirements. The latter is an interesting point, as how many employers could really justify only recruiting 'graduates or similar' for certain jobs? This is a common stipulation in many UK advertisements.

Selection methods

Once candidates have been captured by a recruitment system, the process of gathering detailed personal information begins. This usually starts with each candidate completing an application form or submitting a curriculum vitae (CV). Once these have been checked those candidates who fulfil the initial job requirements are invited for interview. However, in many organizations, there is now an additional stage prior to the interview in which candidates are asked to complete a series of psychometric tests and questionnaires. Sometimes these are combined with other psychological measures to form a one- or two-day assessment process. Such methods are described in Chapter 3.

What differentiates the different ways of gathering information is the objectivity of the selection method. This is a product of how the method is structured and the degree of control the candidate has over the details provided. For example, application forms ask for factual information concerning educational and employment history, but often also give candidates an opportunity to say why they would like a particular job. If candidates answer honestly the first category of information is 'closed', in that the employer is soliciting a certain type of answer, and the second category is 'open' because the candidate can provide whatever information is deemed to be useful. This is in contrast to the CV in which all the information provided is under the candidate's control. Consider also the differences between interviews, questionnaires and psychometric tests. For the first two methods the questions are preplanned and the answers given are at the discretion of the candidate but, with tests, the questions and answer options are fixed. Thus psychometric tests or carefully constructed assessment tasks allow both input and output to be controlled. These distinctions are summarized in Figure 2.1. As you can see, moving from left to right imposes greater structure on the information-collecting methods, and going from top to bottom gives greater control over input and output. Application forms are placed in the middle because they share features with all the other methods.

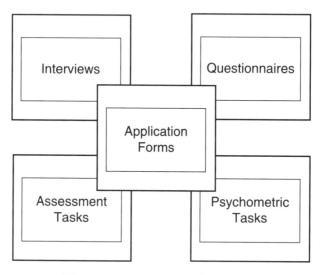

Figure 2.1   Selection methods

Application forms

The application form is one of the most widely used methods of gathering candidate information. In medium- to large-sized organizations they are used for virtually all jobs, apart from very senior positions, although in some public sector organizations – for example the UK National Health Service – they have to be completed by all candidates, including those applying for executive posts.

A typical application form requires candidates to provide the following categories of information:

- **Personal**: name, address, telephone number, nationality and date of birth
- **Educational**: secondary schools, colleges and universities attended, with the dates and any examination results
- **Professional**: membership of any professional organizations, societies or guilds
- **Employment**: previous employers and final positions on leaving; details on responsibilities, achievements and remuneration
- **Interests**: social activities, sports and hobbies
- **Health**: medical conditions which could affect work performance
- **Referees**: two previous employers or professional referees able to supply references
- **Ethnicity**: details of ethnic background required for equal opportunities monitoring

In addition, there may be a section posing a number of open-ended questions concerning the candidate's achievements and aspirations – for example:

- Summarize your main achievements.
- Summarize the major events in your life.
- Why do you want to work for Company X?
- What do you think you can offer Company X?

While it is possible to find questions on these topics on virtually every application form, there are issues concerning their inclusion. The obvious examples are those concerning age, interests and referees. The issue of age is important because, in many circumstances, the candidate's age is (or should be) irrelevant. There may be times when it would be useful to know someone's age, but in most circumstances it is a question which is better not asked, since if there are any problems relating to age these can be tackled later in the selection process, and not at a time when they are likely to lead to irrational and discriminatory judgements. One could also argue that similar considerations apply to any questions which reveal the candidate's gender.

Similarly, questions which ask about a candidate's interests have little bearing on the requirements for most jobs. Perversely, even if they did, the information provided would be of little value because serious candidates take care to include individual and group activities and avoid controversial topics. It is very unlikely that a person would openly provide details on any extreme political activities, illegal sports or addictive habits. This issue of managing the information provided also applies to references. Thus if the candidate is completely free to nominate referees, the names of those supplied can be guaranteed to provide positive reports. In this instance, the only method of counteracting the inevitable is to ensure that the names given are of recent employers, and to use a simple questionnaire to gather information. However, this is only likely to confirm that the candidate worked for the employer in question, plus the dates of employment and any positions held.

The solution to at least some of these problems is to produce different application forms for different jobs, and to make sure that the information requested relates directly to the person specification. If questions have no relationship to the specification, why are they being asked? Worse still, if decisions are made on the basis of information which is irrelevant unsuccessful candidates may well have a case for taking legal action. Therefore, it is a good practice to periodically review application forms and not to rely on a standard form which may well be out-of-date.

Finally, the principal alternative to the application form is the curriculum vitae (CV). This is a method of obtaining information favoured by small organizations and recruitment agencies. However, as a way of systematically comparing candidates it has significant flaws, the obvious one being that, while candidates have an opportunity to 'sell' themselves, they are also at liberty to include and exclude whatever information they wish. This may mean that crucial details which would prevent the candidate from proceeding to the next stage are missing, and entirely irrelevant (yet persuasive) details are included. Furthermore, the way in which the CV is physically presented can influence the assessor's decision and if it has been produced by, say, a professional CV production company, it will give little insight into the candidate. Again, unless an organization is particularly wedded to the CV, or recruits professional staff who are in particularly short supply, a properly constructed application form is probably a better option.

Biodata forms

A biodata form is a special kind of application form which is based on a set of known links between the questions asked and job competencies. Such forms are also used to gather 'soft' information about a candidate's interests, values and aspirations. For example, as well as being asked about educational attainments and employment history, a candidate may have to respond to questions such as the following:

1 Which do you consider to be the most important?

   (a) Skill (b) Intelligence (c) Personality

2 What is your greatest strength?

   (a) Initiative (b) Reliability (c) Ambition (d) Flexibility

These questions obviously demand a personal judgement and differ from those producing a verifiable or 'hard' response. However, whatever the type of questions asked, the principal difference between biodata and applications forms is that the former can be objectively scored. These scores are based on data gathered from existing job incumbents and reflect the differences between 'good' and 'average' employees. Consequently some questions attract higher scores than others, or even negative scores. Unfortunately, while this can lead to the efficient classification of candidates, it can also produce some strange statistical artefacts. For instance, a tendency to criminality has been linked with having a large number of brothers and sisters or lacking a middle name, but because the link is statistical and not causative, it would be extremely unwise to take it at face value!

There are some obvious ethical and privacy problems with the biodata approach, the most significant ones being concerned with indirect discrimination on the grounds of class, race or religion. Thus answers to questions relating to a candidate's siblings may only reflect the cultural origins or religion of his or her parents. Equally, the number of middle names given to a child is often a function of class. This means that biodata forms must be very carefully designed and validated before use.

Biodata information can also be obtained using automatic telephone or computer-based Internet systems in which candidates respond to pre-recorded questions by using the buttons on their telephone or a computer keyboard. Such screening systems have the advantage of being able to cope with thousands of 'calls' and can process candidate information immediately. This leads to large savings in time and money as well as producing a significantly quicker assessment process. The most sophisticated systems allow candidates to book interviews and also coordinate interviewer schedules across sites, or even different parts of a country. Additional benefits for the candidate include the ability to respond from any telephone, or a computer with an Internet link, at any time of day or night.

Automatic systems are widely used in the USA and have proved particularly effective with employers who recruit on a large scale, such as retail organizations and airlines. In the UK and the rest of the EU they are less common, not least because there are problems concerning data protection and the method of selection itself. At the time of writing changes to EU legislation suggest that purely 'automatic' selection will be made illegal and that candidates should always give their prior informed consent. A right of appeal will also be mandatory. Obviously considerations such as these make it important that employers check the legality of any systems they may wish to use.

Selection interviews

This is the most popular method of selecting people for jobs. Many employers consider the interview as the most important part of the selection process, no matter what other tests and assessments are used. Are they right? Unfortunately, the answer is usually 'no', because the average interview is often poorly conducted and does not generate useful selection information. It often concentrates on employment 'chemistry', or whether a person will fit into a particular organization, rather than objectively assessing whether that person has the desired characteristics for performing the job well. In addition, even when interviewers have a more organized approach, their decision-making processes are often erratic. Some common problems are described in Table 2.1.

Table 2.1   Problems with interviews

1 First impressions

Interviewers often make up their minds in the first few minutes of an interview. They then spend the rest of the interview looking for information to confirm their first impressions. This is an example of 'hearing what you want to hear' and results in self-fulfilling decisions.

2· Stereotyping

Interviewers assume that particular characteristics are typical of certain groups – for example, that men with beards are untrustworthy, women who wear glasses are intelligent and Scottish people make good bank managers!

3 Primacy-recency

Interviewers pay more attention to information which emerges early in the interview rather than later. This may be due to a factor of how memory works but is more likely to be the result of the power of first impressions.

4 Contrast effects

Interviewers' ratings of the current candidate are influenced by previous candidates. While this could mean that the best person is selected, it is more likely to distort the process because candidates are only being compared with each other and not against the requirements for the job.

5 Similar-to-me

Interviewers give higher ratings to candidates who have similar backgrounds to their own in terms of upbringing, education and work

Cont.

experience. There is also some evidence that interviewers prefer candi-dates with similar non-verbal behaviour (pattern of eye contact, posture and so on) to their own!

6 Negative information

Interviewers are more influenced by negative information than positive. This is of particular importance if negative information is presented early in the interview as this will lead to a self-fulfilling hunt for further negative information.

7 Personal liking

Interviewers give higher ratings to candidates they like, independent of other job-related factors. This is a natural reaction but perhaps not one that ensures that the best person is selected for a job!

8 Prototyping

Interviewers who favour a particular sort of personality look for it regard-less of job-related factors. This can distort the interview process and lead to candidates with inappropriate personality profiles being selected for jobs.

9 Halo and horns

Interviewers blanket-rate candidates as 'good' (halo) or 'bad' (horns). This makes it particularly difficult to distinguish between those who really are 'good' or 'bad', as there is no comparison made between candidates.

10 Foreign or regional accents

Candidates with foreign or regional accents are often rated less favourably than those with an RP (received pronunciation ('standard') English) accent. However, interestingly, the effect diminishes for 'low-status' jobs, and some regional accents are actually favoured for cus-tomer service jobs.

11 Temporal effects

Interviewers assume that candidates behave in the interview as they do in real life. This is an important error since, for example, it is natural to be more nervous than usual in an interview situation. Conversely, some candidates are very good at putting on an 'act' and pretending to have qualities which they do not possess for the 40 minutes' or so duration of the average interview.

Cont.

12 Gender bias

Interviewers often rate female candidates less favourably than males, especially in male-dominated jobs. However, there is some evidence to suggest that this tendency pertains more to female interviewers than male. For example, female interviewers often rate male candidates as more qualified than female candidates, while the candidate's gender seems to make no difference to male interviewers.

On a more positive note, there are a several ways of radically improving the selection qualities of the interview. The most effective techniques will be explored in the rest of this section, and all of them can be incorporated in interviews whatever their physical format. This includes initial one-to-one and panel interviews, as well as those held at later stages in the selection process.

Different types of interviews

There are a number of ways of structuring the interview. All involve asking candidates the same set of job-related questions. Some also have scoring systems which allow individual responses to be compared to those of the 'ideal' candidate. The traditional method, with which most people are familiar, is based on a verbal examination of a candidate's biography. However, there are other more structured ways of gathering information – namely, behavioural and situational techniques. These are increasing in popularity because they offer a rigorous way of assessing candidates, and can easily be coupled to competency frameworks. The three different types of interview are described below.

Biographical interviews

The biographical interview, which is based on the idea that past behaviour is a good predictor of future behaviour, concentrates on the candidate's past experiences and employment history. When conducted in a structured way it provides a comprehensive picture of a candidate's employment background and style of working. However, the right type of questions must be asked, and care must be taken to treat every candidate in the same way. In practical terms, the questions are based on the 'person specification' which describes the individual characteristics required to successfully perform the job and is constructed using the information gathered through a process of job analysis as described in detail in Chapter 1. In this context, the data will have been used to identify those characteristics which are essential to the performance of the job, those which are non-essential but desirable, and those attributes which may be considered to be contra-indicators. Contra-indicators are factors which would make it impossible to perform the job: for example, in some jobs, less than perfect colour vision.

In terms of process, biographical interviews concentrate on work experience and work style. They explore jobs in reverse chronological order (most recent job first) and are designed to assess the significance of the candidate's current job within the organization, and his or her competence in terms of its requirements. With regard to work style the emphasis is on the candidate's preferred way of dealing with work tasks and colleagues or customers. Indeed, particular attention is often given to assessing supervisory or management potential. The remainder of the interview explores the candidate's aspirations, general education, interests and family background.

After the interview the information provided by the candidate is analysed and judgements are made on such factors as motivation, organizational ability, decision-making, intellectual strength, management ability, flexibility and emotional stability, the latter being concerned with the ability to work under pressure or cope with setbacks and failures.

The advantages of using this type of interview are that it conforms with what candidates expect and is therefore likely to produce the best interview 'performance', and that it can provide a good general picture of a candidate's abilities. However, it also entails a number of problems in that it tends to favour those who are articulate and socially skilled. It also relies heavily on questions being properly related to job criteria. This is a significant point as, in many cases, questions are asked from habit and are in fact irrelevant or, worse still, likely to lead to some form of discrimination. For example, UK employment law would suggest that the following questions should be avoided:

- Where do you come from?
- Where were you born?
- What nationality are your parents?
- What is your religious denomination?
- Are you married?
- Have you any children?
- Where does your spouse work?
- Do you have a disability?

In summary, it is important to plan your questions before the interview and to be mindful of what you can and cannot ask. This should present no problem if you have conducted a thorough job analysis and understand the relevant legislation. It is useful to remember that, as with all laws, ignorance is no defence. Nevertheless, there are ways of legally obtaining certain sorts of information without being blatantly discriminatory or offensive. Thus, whilst you cannot ask if someone is disabled, it is fair to ask 'Do you have any impairments which would interfere with your ability to perform the job for which you have applied, subject to us making any reasonable adjustments?'

If you are in doubt about matters such as these – particularly those concerned with sex discrimination, race relations, disability, rehabilitation of offenders, equal pay and asylum and immigration – obtain copies of the relevant legislation or consult an expert in employment law.

Behavioural interviews

The behavioural, or criterion-referenced interview, is based on structured sets of questions which relate to experiences or abilities in particular job-related areas. The areas (criteria) are derived from a job analysis which has been aimed at identifying the behaviour of 'good' performers. This has allowed the formulation of sets of questions which encourage candidates to provide information which demonstrates that they possess the required behaviours. These are then explored in depth to produce a picture of a candidate's strengths and weaknesses. For example, if it has been shown that the ability to deal with distressed or angry members of the public is an important part of a job, as would be the case with police work, an interviewer would ask questions such as:

- 'Tell me about a time when you had to deal with someone who was very upset'.
- 'What were you trying to achieve?'
- 'What techniques did you use to deal with the situation?'
- 'Why do you think you were successful (unsuccessful)?'
- 'What did you learn from the experience?'
- 'What would you do in a similar situation in the future?'

This sequence of questioning takes a candidate through all the important aspects of a given situation because it asks about the situation itself, what the person was trying to achieve, actions taken and the response to those actions, and the lessons learnt from the whole experience.

The candidate's responses can also be rated against predetermined scales. These are known as 'behaviourally anchored rating scales' (BARS) and are similar to the performance indicators used in competency frameworks. For example, a five-point scale may be used to differentiate between those who do not respond in appropriate ways (low performers) and those who identify needs and respond to them skilfully (high performers). The mid-point would then be indicative of adequate performance. Thus, in the police example above, a low performer would not attempt to find out what was upsetting the person, or would make inaccurate assumptions about the person, leading to inappropriate or mechanistic actions. In contrast, a high performer would identify the cause of the problem and decide on an appropriate and sensitive course of action.

The main strength of the behavioural approach is that it is directly related to the skills that are important to the job. Obviously, it is more relevant to ask a potential police officer about the best way of dealing with a member of the public than use a series of general questions about family background and hobbies. Likewise, it is possible to learn more about a potential salesperson by asking about an occasion when he or she had to give a presentation than by any number of enquiries about school performance or aspects of formal education. Additionally, if a rating scale is used, assessments can be easily compared with those from other sources, such as tests and questionnaires.

On the downside, this form of interviewing can be very time-consuming as it needs to cover all the important aspects of a job. Also, because it concentrates on operational considerations, some aspects of a candidate's background may be overlooked; for example, in some situations – particularly for professional positions – it may be important to thoroughly check out a candidate's educational credentials. Thus it is a technique which is often best combined with an analysis of a candidate's biographical details.

Situational interviews

While biographical and behavioural interviews are based on the assumption that future behaviour is best predicted by past performance, situational interviews rely on the idea that it is best predicted by stated intentions. As a result, the situational interview comprises a series of hypothetical job-related questions, the responses to which are evaluated against a set of model answers. This gives a highly structured interview format that is directly related to work-based scenarios.

The scenarios are often generated using the critical incident technique described in Chapter 1. This has the advantage of collecting information which incumbents feel is important and critical to the successful performance of the job. Scenarios can then be reassessed by all incumbents, and different ways of responding to the situation elicited. These are then classified as 'good', 'bad' and 'poor' responses and allow a rating scale to be constructed. Note, however, that this only works for fairly straightforward situations in which behaviour can be easily classified. If there are a number of equally valid solutions it becomes difficult to devise a scale which allows candidates to be assessed consistently.

This approach is often used in selection for administrative jobs, and has also proved useful with interviews conducted over the telephone. However, the telephone approach does rely on the 'hypothetical' situation being described succinctly and the responses being recorded accurately. That said, questions of the following type have been shown to be good predictors of work behaviour:

■ Question:
'You have delegated some work to a colleague who has done it incorrectly. This has caused a customer to complain. What would you do?'

■ **Responses:**

1 Ignore the situation as customers always complain.
2 Report your colleague to your manager.
3 Contact the customer and resolve the situation.
4 Talk to your colleague and get him to contact the customer.

This method has the advantage that all candidates are asked the same questions and their answers are assessed against a set of fixed responses, thereby producing information of a highly objective nature that allows candidates to be directly compared with each other. In this respect, situational interviews are very much like tests and provide a sound basis for decision-making. However, the method can be seen as challenging and may make some candidates anxious, not least because long questions can be difficult to keep in mind while framing an answer. It has also been suggested that the situational approach actually measures problem-solving skills rather than typical behaviour, and that it favours those with some experience of the job in question.

Summary

There are various ways of structuring interviews. The biographical interview can work well as long as the questions are relevant and are firmly based on the requirements for a job. This implies that the questions should be generated from a job analysis, and it is not sufficient just to use a standard set of questions. With regard to the other two methods, the behavioural approach concentrates on the characteristics of the candidate, and the situational approach on samples of work behaviour. Thus behavioural methods are better suited to those with a short work history or experience in a different work area, such as school-leavers and many graduates. In contrast, situational interviews are more appropriate for candidates seeking new positions in an area with which they are familiar – for example, for those moving from one sales job to another.

There is no doubt that structured interviews are far more effective than informal or unstructured interviews. Indeed, some figures suggest that they are up to three times better at picking 'winners'. However, if this is the case why are unstructured interviews used at all? The answer is fairly straightforward: such interviews require little or no training and allow the interviewer to ask any kind of question. It is also true that it is harder to 'sell' the organization in a structured interview, or to explore how the person will fit into an organization. Whether these are good reasons to perpetuate the unstructured interview depend on your point of view, but surely it is desirable for all candidates to be asked the same questions and for interviewers to be properly trained? The more enlightened organizations ensure that interviewers are practised in key skills such as questioning techniques – in particular using 'open' and 'closed' questions –

establishing rapport, listening, summarizing, reflecting and controlling the information flow.

The results of personality questionnaires (see Chapter 3) can also be used to generate objectively based questions which can be asked at interview. An extract from an example report is presented at the end of the chapter (see pp 44–7).

Interview checklist

Preparing for the interview:

- Conduct a behavioural job analysis.
- Produce a person specification.
- Select an appropriate interview method.
- Ensure that you are properly trained.
- Compile a series of job-related questions.

During the interview:

- Ensure that you ask all of your questions.
- Consider equal opportunities and similar issues.
- Obtain focused job-related information.
- Avoid predictable interviewer 'problems'(see Table 2.1, p. 36).
- Record pertinent information as you proceed.

After the interview:

- Evaluate evidence against original job requirements.
- Combine findings with other objective information, for example, tests.
- Record reasons why candidates were selected.
- Record reasons why candidates were *not* selected.
- Continually re-evaluate your interview style.

Using recruitment and interview techniques

The production of a tightly worded recruitment advertisement and its placement in the most appropriate media are skilled tasks. Employers who have limited experience of this sort of activity are well advised to seek the assistance of a recruitment professional. This becomes particularly important for senior and professional level positions, as the services of a 'head-hunter' (executive search agency) may well be required. In the

UK details of firms offering recruitment services can be found in a number of standard references – for example, *The Personnel Manager's Yearbook* (AP Information Services).

With regard to application forms these need to be very carefully constructed with an eye on the relevant legislation. A good basic introduction to employment law is provided by Erich Suter's book, *Employment Law Checklist* (London: IPD), as this provides a chronological list of legislation with summaries of the contents, scope and effects of each Act. However, as with all things legal, if in doubt seek professional help. Indeed, if you are considering the use of biodata forms you will definitely need to retain the services of a business psychologist and have the contents doublechecked by an employment law specialist. Biodata form design is a technical activity which is best left to the experts.

Again, it is wise to consider what sort of questions can be legitimately asked in an interview situation. Most interviewers should have little problem with the biographical approach as long as it is related to an up-to-date person specification. Nevertheless, it is very easy to conduct a poor interview, so skills training for all interviewers should be the order of the day. The two more complicated techniques, the behavioural and situational approaches, can be delivered by trained interviewers but do depend on the drafting of appropriate questions and the construction of rating scales. In most organizations the latter will require work by a business psychologist. Interview prompt systems, such as those driven by personality questionnaires, generally also involve the services of a psychologist, although they can be used by personnel who have successfully completed the correct form of training (see Chapter 3 for details on psychometric test training courses).

Example 16PF5™ interview prompts*

Screentest 16PF Interview Prompts

General style of relating to people

1 Interest in people and enjoyment of group activities
The responses suggest that a high level of enjoyment is derived from being with and working with others. Less satisfaction is likely to be gained from solitary pursuits or working alone. Questions might relate to feelings about these less preferred areas and the strategies used to deal with them. For example:

■ Under what conditions have you made a decision without consulting others?
■ How do you maintain your concentration?

*Copyright © NFER-Nelson 1993. This extract is from the *Screentest Sixteen Personality Questionnaire Interview Prompts* report produced by ASE, a division of NFER-Nelson. It is reproduced by permission of the publishers, NFER-Nelson, Darville House, 2 Oxford Road East, Windsor, Berkshire SL4 1DF, UK.

2 Openness

[Name] has described herself through the questions as someone who prefers to be forthright and straightforward with others. The risk is that this may be seen by some as lack of tact. Questioning might explore the extent to which [name] takes account of the impact of the way she expresses things. For example:

- How important is it to be forthright in the way you express things at work?
- In what situations at work do you control your natural desire to say what you think?
- Plain speaking can often help to move projects along and cut through resistance. How has your preference for speaking your mind helped you at work? In what situations have you found it less useful?
- Your responses to the questionnaire suggest that you are forthright. What advantages and disadvantages have you experienced with this?

3 Vigilance

The way the questions have been answered suggest that [name's] first inclination would be to accept what other people say and do as being sincere rather than questioning their motives. This can have a positive impact on group morale. The danger is that because of her easy acceptance of people at face value, she may be taken advantage of. Questions might explore the extent to which [name's] acceptance may lead her to misread signs that there is cause for mistrusting a person. For example:

- Most businesses are based to some extent on trust. What are the disadvantages of this that you have seen at work?
- What have you found to be the dangers of trusting people too much too soon? How have you avoided doing that?
- How have you dealt with being let down by a colleague?
- Tell me about a time when you mistrusted a colleague.

4 Desire to influence

Responses to the questions give the impression that [name] has a tendency to put other people's needs and wishes above her own. [Name] may not always stand up for herself. There might be a tendency to say yes to unreasonable demands. Questioning might relate to the need for supervision, the style of supervision preferred, how [name] deals with unstructured time, how opportunities for using initiative have been dealt with and how [name] responds to unreasonable demands. It might also be useful to explore the degree to which the environment influences the likelihood of [name] stating her opinions and expressing her needs. In addition questions might explore the manner in which [name] gets her views and needs across. For example:

- Tell me about a time that you have had a problem and had to confront others with it.
- In what situations, in and outside work, do you feel most comfortable about standing up for yourself?
- How do you like to be managed? To what extent do you need supervision?

5 Social boldness

The way the questions have been answered suggests that [name] may feel less at ease than most when singled out for attention. She may feel more comfortable when familiar with a situation or when with people she knows well. Questioning might explore how her tendency to be self conscious manifests itself and whether anything is avoided because of shyness. You might explore [name's] preferred method for communicating at work and the effectiveness of it. For example:

■ Tell me about a situation in your current job where you have had to tell somebody something they would rather not have heard.
■ When it comes to communicating with others what would you say are your greatest strengths? What aspects of your communication skills would you like to improve?
■ What is your preferred method for communicating at work?
■ What aspects of your work do you enjoy most?

6 Liveliness
The responses suggest that [name] is as lively and enthusiastic about things as most people. Questioning might explore the particular types of activities and tasks that stimulate [name's] enthusiasm and interest. For example:

■ What 'turns you on' most at work? And what 'turns you off'?
■ What aspects of your current job do you find boring?
■ Enthusiasm and boredom are often part of office life. How do you balance them?
■ Do you finish as many projects as you start? How easy do you find it to maintain your enthusiasm?

Thinking style

1 Focus of attention when taking in information
[Name] appears to achieve balance between responding to what is immediately apparent or necessary and considering the broader view or the implications of what is known. Questioning might be aimed at clarifying the nature of the balance. For example:

■ How often do you find yourself getting bogged down in and distracted by the fine detail of a project? How much time would you normally spend on acquainting yourself with the finer details?
■ Do your colleagues describe you as more of a thinker or more of a 'doer'? What is more important at work?
■ How much of your job involves you in the discussion of ideas? Would you like it to take up more or less of your time?
■ How easy do you find it to move between considering the fine detail and thinking broadly? Which do you tend to do more of?

2 Objectivity
The way the questions have been answered suggests an enjoyment of the more aesthetic side of life rather than its more practical or factual aspects. [Name] is a person whose feelings about things are likely to influence her judgements so she is less likely to be purely objective or hard-headed about issues. Questions will most usefully relate to the way [name] evaluates information but it may be difficult for her to describe her own thinking style. So it may be easier to explore this aspect from a values perspective: that is to say the relative importance attached to emotional aspects of life on the one hand and more concrete practical aspects on the other. For example:

■ What do you value most in your friends?

■ Being aware of the emotional issues involved in a decision may have advantages at times and disadvantages at others? What have you found the advantages and disadvantages to be?
■ Describe a situation in which you have been prepared to make a decision based mainly on a gut feeling that it was right?
■ Please describe a situation where you had to make a decision which had harsh implications for yourself or others? What effect did this have on you?

3 Orientation to change

Responses suggest that [name] is as open to change as most. Probably she holds some traditional values and has a certain respect for tried and tested methods but remains open to new ways of looking at things and to potential improvements to existing systems. Questions might explore typical strategies for dealing with change and the likelihood of initiating it. For example:

■ How often do you make changes to the way you do things at work?
■ When you first began your current job, what was the most challenging aspect of the transition for you?
■ How quickly do you tend to adjust to the changes at work? Please give examples.
■ The need to change and the need for stability are often part of working life. How do you feel about the balance of these in your work at the moment?

Note: Further sections would cover 'consistency of performance' and 'management of pressure'.

Further information

Anderson, N. and Shakleton, V. (1993), *Successful Selection Interviewing,* Oxford: Blackwell.
Courtis, J. (1994), *Recruitment Advertising – Right First Time,* London: IPD.
Gunter, B., Furnham, A. and Drakely, R. (1993), *Biodata: Biographical Indicators of Business Performance*, London: Routledge.
Hackett, P. (1995), *The Selection Interview,* London: IPD.

Psychometrics and Assessment Centres

Overview

Psychometric tests and questionnaires provide one of the most efficient ways of discovering what a person is like. As long as they are carefully matched to the requirements for a job they also provide good evidence of individual potential and likely work performance. This is why they are routinely used by over 80 per cent of major UK employers. A similar figure is found in North America, with tests also forming a significant part of the selection process in most EU countries and many parts of the southern hemisphere. This chapter reviews the different sorts of tests and questionnaires and gives guidance on their use.

A closely related selection activity, the assessment centre, is also explored. This involves the integration of tests and questionnaires with other forms of assessment and is a popular method of selecting graduates, middle managers and senior executives. Details are given on the range of assessment exercises which can be used and how assessment centres are organized.

Psychometric measures form an important part of many interventions in business psychology as they generate high-quality, focused information. However, as they must be used by appropriately skilled personnel, the issue of training is a prime concern. For this reason, details are provided on UK training requirements.

Psychometric tests

Psychometric tests provide an objective way of measuring particular aspects of human behaviour. These include a wide range of abilities and other individual characteristics, such as personality, values and interests.

Individual tests are carefully constructed so that every candidate who takes one encounters identical questions under the same carefully controlled conditions. Consequently they are administered according to a set of detailed instructions, describing how an individual should approach the test, how long there will be to complete the questions, and other related issues. Other parts of the process are also standardized, particularly the method of marking the answers and the interpretation which can be placed on the results.

The entire testing process is designed to provide objective information which can be used to directly compare one person with another, or to give a measure of an individual's pattern of strengths and limitations. As such, it provides information which empowers the selection process and adds value to other assessment methods, such as the interview. For example, many managers feel uneasy about making hiring decisions on the basis of an interview alone; the use of tests can help to complete the picture and allow more informed judgements to be made.

Test quality

Whether or not a psychometric test provides useful information depends on the context in which it is used and on the quality of its construction. The context relies on being able to identify the behavioural requirements of a job and the quality on the test's design. The latter is a detailed and lengthy process which ensures that tests produce information which is fair, reliable, valid and predictive.

■ **Fair**. Tests should not discriminate unfairly in terms of race, culture, gender or any other similar factor. Obviously there will be differences in performance but these must be due to real differences in the attribute being measured, and not just to the way in which the test is constructed.

■ **Reliable**. A test must consistently measure the same attribute across time without being influenced by irrelevant factors. Thus a person tested with the same test (or two equivalent versions) on two separate occasions should produce comparable results. Technically this is known as establishing test–retest reliability.

■ **Valid**. A test must measure what it is supposed to measure. For example, a test of numerical reasoning would be expected to measure some aspect of arithmetical or mathematical ability and, not for instance, verbal ability. This is an important point and goes beyond the 'look' of a test (face validity). It rests on being able to demonstrate that a test produces results which correlate with another measure of the same attribute.

■ **Predictive**. A test must be an accurate predictor of future performance. In a selection context this is crucial because tests are generally used to identify, from a pool of candidates, those who are likely to perform better at a particular job. To do this it is necessary to establish that a test actually does predict performance by correlating test results with measures of performance (predictive validity). Performance measures can include such factors as appraisal ratings and sales figures.

In summary, a great deal of effort is put into establishing that tests work effectively and that they measure factors which are directly relevant to specific employment situations. Publishers also ensure that appropriate training is available for test users, and that up-to-date information is provided so that employers can make fully informed decisions.

What can tests measure?

Tests can be classified in a number of different ways but they usually measure either maximum or typical performance. Maximum performance concerns how well an individual can do something – for example, use numerical information – and typical performance how a person is likely to 'behave' at home or at work. From a test point of view the first category includes all forms of ability testing, and the second includes measures of personality and similar characteristics.

Ability tests

There are tests available which can measure over 50 different abilities. These cover the cognitive abilities such as verbal or mechanical reasoning, psychomotor abilities like hand-eye coordination, physical abilities relating to speed, stamina and strength, and sensory abilities like, for instance, vision and hearing. As a result there are about 4500 ability tests on the market, most of which are designed for English-speaking countries. However, despite the number of tests available, those used for selection and development tend to fall into the following categories:

■ **Abstract** – the ability to solve new problems from first principles. This is also known as 'general intelligence' with tests of this sort providing an indication of a candidate's intellectual power. Abstract reasoning tests can also furnish results in the form of an Intelligence Quotient (IQ), which is the ratio of a candidate's mental age to his or her chronological age. The questions in general intelligence tests are often based on symbols and not verbal or numerical concepts; this ensures that the only way to solve the problems is to work them out from scratch.
■ **Verbal** – the ability to reason with verbal or written information. There are many aspects of ability which can be measured from spelling, grammar and the meaning of words to verbal critical reasoning. However, it is important with all verbal tests to ensure that the level of language is appropriate for the candidate group, especially with those for which English is not a first language. An example of a verbal critical reasoning test is provided in Table 3.1.

Table 3.1   Example test questions

Verbal critical reasoning

Read the passage below and decide whether the statements which follow are true, false or if you cannot tell.

'Shark attacks, and injuries inflicted by big cats and other carnivores, can result in serious tissue damage. In such circumstances the most important thing to do is to stop the bleeding as quickly as possible. Nothing you or a physician can do will be of any use if the victim bleeds to death. In the case of injuries inflicted by a shark, the prevention of a massive haemorrhage is about all anyone can do, although it is equally important to treat the shock.'

1 Big cats and other carnivores are dangerous animals.
2 It is important to treat shock before stopping any bleeding.
3 Shark attacks can lead to massive haemorrhaging.

Numerical critical reasoning

Using the information provided answer the questions which follow. You may not use a calculator.

Graduate numbers in various types of training over a three-year period

	Year 1	Year 2	Year 3
Personnel	5000	6500	7200
Finance	6500	12300	14500
Administration	3300	4100	4900
Production	1500	1700	2100
Quality	230	432	640
Sales	6700	7705	9800

1 How many graduates are likely to be in Administration training in Year 4?

(a) 5600   (b) 5400   (c) 5700   (d) 5500   (e) 5900

2 What is the percentage increase in Sales training over the first two years?

(a) 13.5%   (b) 14%   (c) 14.5%   (d) 15%   (e) 15.5%

3 What proportion of Year 1 graduates were in Quality training compared to those in all other types of training?

(a) 1%   (b) 0.1%   (c) 1.5%   (d) 0.8%   (e) cannot tell

■ **Numerical** – the ability to reason with numerical or quantitative data. As with verbal tests, there are many things which can be measured, from simple arithmetic ability to higher mathematics. In a selection context, numerical tests are available which assess a candidate's ability to deal with the sort of information which is typical of a business scenario. An example of a numerical critical reasoning test is provided in Table 3.1.

■ **Diagrammatic** – the ability to reason with diagrammatic or symbolic information. Tests can be used which measure a number of aspects of diagrammatic skill, from the ability to follow instructions presented in a symbolic form to the use of symbols in fault-finding. A typical question would involve the candidate using a key, which describes the functions of a range of symbols, to solve a problem based on a flow-chart.

■ **Spatial** – the ability to mentally manipulate objects in two and three-dimensional space. Spatial tests are concerned with measuring a candidate's ability to compare two shapes, recognize complex shapes, or decipher shapes which have been rotated or reversed. An example of the type of question used in this sort of test is one that presents the candidate with a series of two-dimensional plans for a three-dimensional object. The task is to decide which plan can be used to produce the object.

■ **Mechanical** – the ability to use mechanical and physical principles to solve problems. Mechanical tests measure a candidate's ability to interpret visual representations of simple 'machines', or to understand the mechanical principles governing structures (stress and strain), energy (heat, light and power) or forces (gravity, centrifugal and centripetal forces).

■ **Checking** – the ability to check detailed information quickly without making mistakes. Checking or classification tests concentrate on the speedy and accurate checking of verbal and numerical information. The test 'questions' are presented as two sets of information which require differences to be highlighted.

■ **Dexterity** – the ability to accurately manipulate objects or tools with the hands. This is a combination of manual speed and skill and is usually assessed with a simple 'construction' task. For example, candidates can be asked to place washers on pins and place them in holes on a board, or to construct an object from a series of given components using a schematic plan for guidance.

It is important to realise that, within many of the categories mentioned, it is possible to measure both attainment (knowledge) and aptitude (potential). For example, a verbal attainment test might measure accuracy of spelling or the appreciation of grammar, whereas a verbal aptitude test would be concerned with understanding the relationship between words, or the logic of verbal arguments. In this way, attainment tests are useful for establishing what a person already knows, and aptitude tests what an individual might be able to do in the future.

Other sorts of test include trainability tests and business learning exercises. Trainability tests are designed to assess whether a person can be trained to perform a particular task. For example, a garment manufacturer may use a test which involves giving a candidate instructions on sewing the pocket on to a pair of trousers and then testing whether the instructions are followed with a real pair of trousers. Tests of this type are often used for jobs which require the use of machinery or the completion of practical tasks.

Business learning exercises represent an integrated approach to psychometric assessment. They differ from traditional tests, which measure individual abilities, in that they are based on complete problem scenarios. The tests work by leading you through a number of tasks which teach you what to do, and then by finding out how you apply what you have learnt in practice. A typical scenario might be that you are a customer service agent and you have to deal with a range of enquiries from the public. The information you need is contained in a number of manuals and what you can say is governed by a set of procedures. Your task is to deliver the correct information with regard to the procedures which apply across a number of different situations.

Exercises like these present realistic situations which require the candidate to use a number of different abilities. In many ways, such exercises are a fairer method of assessment because they make no prior assumptions about the candidate's knowledge base – all the information required, and the 'rules' governing its use, is provided within the exercise. Over the next few years, tests of this sort will become more widely used, particularly for selecting customer service and sales personnel. The leading practitioners in this area are Oxford Psychologists Press which publish a range of assessments under the title *Aptitude for Business Learning Exercises* (ABLE).

Selecting the right test

Once the need for psychometric testing has been identified it is necessary to obtain information on the appropriate tests by contacting test publishers and finding out whether they have products which meet your requirements. In most situations you will be presented with a range of options involving the use of different combinations of tests. For example, in graduate selection it is usual to measure verbal and numerical ability; whereas in engineering, verbal, numerical, diagrammatic, spatial and mechanical ability may be assessed. These different combinations of tests are called 'test batteries'. To make the point, Table 3.2 illustrates the sort of tests

Table 3.2   Using ability tests

Ability tests		Candidate groups					
		Clerical/ Admin	Process/ Manufacturing	Technical/ Engineering	Marketing/ Sales	Computing/ IT	Graduate/ Managerial
Verbal	Spelling	*					*
	Grammar	*					*
	Word meanings	*	*	*	*	*	*
	Following instructions	*	*	*	*	*	*
	Critical reasoning	*		*	*	*	*
Numerical	Arithmetic	*	*	*		*	*
	Estimating	*	*	*	*	*	
	Data entry	*				*	
	Data evaluation	*			*	*	*
	Critical reasoning	*		*	*	*	*
Diagrammatic	Using symbolic data	*	*	*		*	
	Fault finding		*	*			
	Critical reasoning	*		*		*	*
Spatial	Visual comparisons		*	*			
	Two-dimensional reasoning		*	*		*	*
	Three-dimensional reasoning		*	*		*	*
Mechanical	Mechanical comprehension		*	*			
	Manual assembly		*	*			
Checking	Checking text or data	*	*	*		*	
	Classifying data	*	*	*		*	

which are routinely used with different candidate groups. All can be obtained from major test publishers worldwide. A list of key contacts is provided at the end of this book.

The two short case studies which follow illustrate the use of ability tests in different contexts.

Case study: Selecting process operators

A subsidiary of a large Swiss chemical company, which specialized in the production of food flavourings and fragrances, decided to relocate its production facility within the UK. As part of the relocation the existing workforce were all offered jobs in the new plant. However, a number decided not to move and so additional staff were required.

The company employed a consultant who analysed the tasks performed by the process operators and designed a selection process to assess new staff. This involved the use of two tests which were used in advance of a short interview and which measured the ability to understand and apply written instructions (important for following production formulae) and apply basic arithmetic to process tasks (crucial for measuring and weighing materials). The assessments mirrored the needs of the company's quality assurance programme as, in the past, problems had arisen because of the inaccurate use of raw materials – a serious issue when the nature of a flavour or fragrance can be badly affected by a small inaccuracy in a recipe.

In all, 45 candidates were tested, with 15 subsequently selected for interview. After the interviews six candidates were offered jobs. The same organization used a combination of interviews, tests and a personality questionnaire to select a number of graduate trainees. In this case, the tests were designed to measure critical reasoning, decision-making ability and planning style; the questionnaire assessed interpersonal skills, team mindedness, action-orientation and resilience.

Case study: Selecting commercial airline pilots

A major UK pilot training organization decided to revise its candidate assessment process by using a series of psychometric tests. These were picked on the basis of a detailed job specification, with the aim of classifying candidates according to their training 'risk' – an important consideration when the basic training for each successful candidate costs in excess of £50 000.

The initial selection of candidates, with often over 500 applying for each position, is based on them being between the ages of 18 and 26 with a minimum of two 'A' Levels and five GCSEs. Those who fulfil the criteria then attend an orientation day, with a second day assigned to a comprehensive series of tests comprising the ability to reason from first principles, high-level general ability with an emphasis on numerical and perceptual aptitude, practicality, and a flexible and confident problem-solving style. A second series of specialist tests, measuring physical co-ordination, the ability to apply verbal instructions to visual tasks and sim-ulations of aircraft take-offs and landings are also used.

The use of two sets of tests, an interview and, ultimately, a full medical ensures that only those candidates with a high probability (low training risk) of completing the course are selected. The system continues to be used on candidates applying for positions with airlines such as Virgin Atlantic, Caledonian Airways, Air 2000 and Jersey European.

Personality questionnaires

Personality plays an important part in how a person performs in a work setting. Indeed, as it is of central importance in all those situations which involve direct interaction with other people, measures of personality are valuable for selecting individuals for all forms of managerial, supervisory, customer service, sales, team- or group-based activities. When used in conjunction with information on abilities and occupational interests, information about personality is also particularly useful for staff development or careers guidance.

The elements of personal style which constitute personality are often measured using a self-report questionnaire. This is a paper-and-pencil assessment, or a series of questions presented on a computer screen, which asks about the ways in which a person typically thinks or behaves. The questions relate to a number of distinct aspects (dimensions) of personality.

Interestingly, after much debate, most psychologists now agree that there are five dimensions – colloquially known as the 'Big Five' – of particular importance. They account for all observable behaviour and concern how people: behave towards others' (relating); approach new situations (action); control their emotions (feelings); regulate their actions (conformity); reason (think). More specifically, they can be described as:

- **Extroversion** – how a person reacts towards other people.
- **Tough-mindedness** – the way in which a person goes about getting things done.
- **Anxiety** – how relaxed and comfortable a person is internally.
- **Independence** – how a person responds to variety and change.
- **Self-organization** – the way in which a person structures and controls life.

The questions in personality questionnaires can be presented in a number of different ways, but the most usual method is to offer candidates either a choice of responses such as 'Yes', 'No' and '?'(Unsure), or a more complex five-grade system. Such grading systems allow candidates to indicate if they strongly agree (1) or disagree (5) with a statement, or just agree (2) or disagree (4). As before, there is a midpoint (3) which can be used if a candidate is unsure. Some examples are given below:

Example 1
1 Are you always late for appointments?   [Yes]   [?]   [No]
2 Do you plan your work well in advance?   [Yes]   [?]   [No]
3 Are you comfortable in social situations? [Yes]   [?]   [No]

Example 2
1 Do you take the lead in discussions?   [1] [2] [3] [4] [5]
2 Do you prefer tried-and-tested methods?   [1] [2] [3] [4] [5]
3 Should people sort out their own problems? [1] [2] [3] [4] [5]

An additional feature of most questionnaires is a series of questions which are designed to detect if candidates are trying to present themselves in an overly positive way. This is, of course, a perfectly natural behaviour in this context, but, if it is not recognized, it does tend to distort the results. These special questions provide information on what is called 'impression management' or 'motivational distortion'.

There are fewer personality questionnaires than ability tests on the market, but estimates suggest that there are still about 1200 to choose from! However, the market is dominated by three particular question-naires. The most popular is the *Sixteen Personality Factor Questionnaire*™ (16PF™) published in the USA by the Institute for Personality and Ability Testing, Inc. This is a 'Big Five' questionnaire but, as the name implies, it divides the main dimensions into 16 different scales. It is available in different languages and can be obtained in the UK from ASE. The remaining two questionnaires are the *Occupational Personality Questionnaire*® (OPQ®), published in the UK by Saville & Holdsworth Ltd, and the *California Psychological Inventory*™ (CPI™) published in the USA by the Consulting Psychologists Press, Inc. The OPQ comprises a family of questionnaires with the most sophisticated version measuring personality on 30 different scales. As with the 16PF, it is available in a range of different languages. Likewise, the CPI, which is available in the UK from Oxford Psychologists Press, is available in a number of forms measuring up to 23 different aspects of personality.

As mentioned, personality questionnaires are widely used in selection for jobs which have a strong interpersonal element. They can also provide useful information on aspects of innovation. Indeed, one area of growing importance is the use of questionnaires to assist in the selection of corpo-rate entrepreneurs, or those who are sometimes called 'intrepreneurs'. Research in this area with the OPQ has shown that intrepreneurs are less controlling and modest and more artistic, less traditional and less concerned with detail than most managers. They are also more conceptual, forward planning and achieving. All this suggests that intrepreneurs are more open to new ideas and have a greater strategic vision than the average manager. Such findings help to provide a 'template' for selecting innovators. A similar approach can, of course, be used for any other situation in which aspects of personality are seen as playing a principal role in job performance.

Test administration and interpretation

Tests and questionnaires are administered under carefully controlled conditions. This involves the selection of a suitable test environment, a quiet room with sufficient space for all the candidates to work without distraction, and strict adherence to the instructions and timings laid down by the test publisher. All this ensures that everyone is treated in the same way and that the results from each candidate can be compared one with another. Another way of ensuring equal treatment is to send candidates practice tests in advance of the assessment session. These are produced by most of the major test publishers and are a good way of preparing candidates for the real assessment.

The test materials are usually in the form of question books and separate answer papers. This allows candidates to record their answers in pencil and for the answer sheets to be automatically scored using an optical mark reading system. It is also possible to administer tests on a PC or using a 'palm-top' computer. However, this relies on an organization having access to sufficient computers and it is therefore a method which is difficult to use with large numbers of candidates. Additionally, some tests can be administered over the Internet. This is an exciting development as it opens up the possibility of 'remote testing' or being able to assess candidates without them having to report to a particular location. Nevertheless there are problems, not least the availability of equipment, and also ensuring that the right person does the test.

When a candidate has completed a series of tests the first step is to mark them and produce what are called raw scores. These are simply the number of questions answered correctly or in the case of a questionnaire, the number of responses which relate to a specific dimension or scale. The next step is to compare the results with a suitable normative group – namely a representative sample of people who have completed the test or questionnaire in the past, such as a sample of the general UK population or occupational groups such as engineers, sales professionals or different types of managers. The process of comparison allows raw scores to be converted to the scaled scores which allow candidates to be objectively compared with each other. Scaled scores can be expressed in a number of different ways but the most common is to describe the results in terms of percentiles. Thus if a candidate scores at the 80th percentile, this is better than 80 per cent of the normative group or, to put it another way, the candidate is in the top 20 per cent.

After the test results have been standardized they can be used in a number of different ways. The three main approaches are 'top-down' and 'bottom-up' selection, or profiling. With top-down selection the top scorers are selected, from the highest downwards, until the available positions have been filled. This may seem to be the most logical approach but it does incur a number of problems. First, it assumes that the top scorers are actually achieving a suitable level of performance for the job in question whereas, in reality, none of the candidates may be performing at a high enough standard. Second, and in complete contrast to the first point, if candidates really are performing at a high level, such a level of performance may not be necessary. It is not unusual for organizations to pick those with high scores only to find that they become bored with jobs which require a lower level of performance.

The alternative is to use the 'bottom-up' approach which involves setting a minimum level of performance – a point above which candidates have to score if they are to be selected. This solves some of the problems of the 'top-down' approach but relies on an organization being able to identify cut-off points. This is possible with existing jobs because current employees can be tested, but it does pose a problem if testing is aimed at selection for a new position.

Finally, the most sophisticated approach is to profile the results against the requirements for a job. This involves taking account of the relative balances of test result against each other. It is also a way of highlighting the strengths and weaknesses of individual candidates. For example, many managerial jobs require more verbal and numerical ability than diagrammatic, whereas medical positions demand more verbal and diagrammatic than numerical. The identification of patterns like these allows for more efficient selection and also draws attention to candidates who have achieved good scores but not on the 'right' tests.

The last part of the interpretation process involves the production of a written report. This can be in the form of a short set of notes which describe the tests or questionnaires completed, the scores obtained and the implications in terms of the person specification, or as a detailed narrative which explores the results in considerable depth. Such narratives are typical of personality questionnaires because of the complexity of the subject matter. To illustrate the point, an example report is reproduced on pp 73–6.

The production of reports allows employers to provide feedback to test candidates. This is a key part of testing if tests or questionnaires are used for development purposes, as you will see later in this book, but of less importance in a selection context since it is often impractical to feed back test results to many people, especially as the majority will not have secured a position. However, on purely ethical grounds, many employers do offer limited feedback to unsuccessful candidates as it can help with their preparation for other job applications. It is also a good PR exercise and helps project the organization in a positive and caring way.

Testing in different languages

Tests are available in a wide range of different languages. However, converting a test from one language to another, and then using it in a different country, is not a straightforward matter. In particular, problems can arise in translation, especially with translations from English to languages with smaller vocabularies. A case in point would be the production of a French version of an English verbal test because there are about 200 000 English words in common use, whereas in French there are only 100 000. This makes it very difficult to produce 'identical' tests. The physical space that words occupy can also cause problems – German, for instance, takes up about a third more room than English. In other languages different problems arise because the 'words' say too much. This is especially true of ideographic languages such as Chinese, Japanese and Korean. A classic example is the question in a mechanical ability test which asks:

Q. What device changes the voltage of a power supply?
A. (a) Rectifier (b) Battery (c) Alternator (d) Transformer

This works well in English but the Chinese characters which make up the word 'transformer' mean 'change voltage apparatus'! This suggests that tests need to be very carefully translated and that it is impossible just to directly substitute one word or character for another. Similar problems can arise with languages which are very similar, such as American and British English. For example, the meaning of the words 'duplex', 'trunk', 'pacifier', 'yard' and 'crosswalk' are all immediately obvious to an American but less so to someone from Britain. Interestingly, even when words or situations are used which are common to two 'languages', the psychological reaction to them can be quite different. Take the case of the personality questionnaire item:

At times, I feel like starting an argument with someone   [True]   [False]

In the UK 87 per cent of men and 86 per cent of women answer 'true' to this question, but in the USA the distribution is 42 per cent of men and 24 per cent of women. The contrast is marked and highlights fundamental differences between British and American respondents with regard to this item, which is actually a measure of aggressiveness. Interestingly, UK men and women seem to be equally aggressive, whereas American men are far more likely to want to start an argument than American women. All this emphasizes an important point – namely, that it is vital that tests are renormed on the target population. If they are not, and results are not compared with an appropriate group, it is easy to wildly under- or over-estimate aspects of a person's personality. Unfortunately, renorming is an extremely time-consuming process as it involves testing hundreds, if not thousands, of people, but it does mean that it is possible to compare like with like. While the example above shows that it is dangerous to assume that Americans are like Britains, there are even greater differences between other cultures. The moral is obvious, if you need to use tests prepared in different languages make sure you consult a reputable test publisher with international experience.

Training in test use

In order to get the best out of psychometric tests it is necessary to be trained in their use. In the UK this involves undertaking one of the training courses prescribed by the British Psychological Society (BPS). The two main programmes which are available lead to certification in the use of occupational tests at Level-A and Level-B standard. Level-A courses concern the use of ability tests and concentrate on the theory of ability testing, the statistics behind test construction, deciding when tests should be used, and the practicalities of test administration, scoring and interpretation. The Level-B course covers similar topics, but as applied to personality questionnaires and similar measures. Both courses last for five or six days and involve considerable individual work.

On successful completion of a Level-A course a manager will have access to a wide range of ability tests, although some test publishers will insist on additional training or familiarization with their products before they are made available. The situation with Level-B training is slightly more complicated as the qualification gives access to the questionnaires studied on the course, but not to the full range of personality measures. It is also available at a 'full' and 'intermediate' level; this means that if a manager wishes to use other questionnaires, further 'conversion' training will be required.

Outside the UK a number of countries operate similar systems. There are also international guidelines on the competencies required for test use, the best known being those published by the American Psychological Association and the International Test Commission. These cover issues which are of universal importance such as the fair and non-discriminatory use of tests and the confidentiality of tests results. The latter is an important consideration in EU countries because of data protection legislation.

Test checklist

Before the test session:

- Produce a behavioural person specification.
- Identify those attributes which can be tested.
- Decide on appropriate tests and/or questionnaires.
- Check the reliability and validity of tests and/or questionnaires.
- Check the equal opportunities implications.
- Decide on the delivery method (paper-and-pencil or computer).
- Obtain practice tests for candidates, if available.
- Decide on how the tests will be administered (to groups or individuals).
- Nominate a trained person to administer the tests.
- Select a suitable test location.

During the test session:

- Explain the testing process to the candidates.
- Allow candidates to ask questions about the process.
- Ensure that the tests are administered according to their instructions.
- Keep a log of each test session and record any unusual events.
- Collect all materials at the end of the session.
- Explain to the candidates what will happen next.

After the test session:

- Mark the tests according to the publisher's instructions.
- Make sure that you use appropriate norms.
- Use a top-down, bottom-up or profiling approach.
- Integrate the information with other measures, if appropriate.
- Keep the test results confidential and secure.
- Provide feedback to candidates, if appropriate.
- Retain test information in line with any relevant legislation.

Assessment centres

One of the most powerful ways of assessing candidates is to systematically use a number of different measures. In practice, this involves combining the results of interviews and paper-and-pencil assessments with those from a number of job simulation exercises. Such an approach, which combines information from a number of different sources, is the basis of the 'assessment centre'.

As well as the use of a range of assessments, the assessment centre is characterized by the fact that each candidate is evaluated by more than one assessor. This is an important feature because the involvement of a number of trained assessors increases the objectivity and impartiality of the process. Another unique characteristic is that groups of candidates are assessed together. This allows assessors to observe behaviour in a more natural setting and to use genuinely interactive assessment tasks. However, it should be evident that the combination of a number of candidates, assessment methods and assessors makes assessment centres both time-consuming and expensive. Nevertheless research shows that this sort of multi-method approach is by far the most valid way of assessing candidates for jobs. As a result, assessment centres are now widely used for selection purposes, especially for graduate and managerial jobs. Indeed the Industrial Relations Service estimates that over half the medium- to large-sized organizations in the UK use some form of assessment centre. A similar picture emerges in many other Western countries, with the approach being at its most developed in the USA.

The assessment centre is typically run over one or two days and often necessitates candidates being accommodated overnight. In addition, it requires some very careful preparation as each candidate and assessor needs to know precisely what is happening throughout the assessment process. This may just be a question of simple logistics but many assessment centres fail to produce the best possible results because of administrative problems. That said, the great advantage of the assessment centre is its flexibility and that different combinations of assessment methods can be used for different jobs. For this reason there are likely to be significant differences between one assessment centre and another. This makes it vital that they are properly planned and appropriate measures selected.

Designing an assessment centre

The first step of the design process is to establish the key job requirements. As discussed previously, this is a question of job analysis and is a step which cannot be omitted. It should also be apparent that, as assessment centres are geared to measuring aspects of behaviour, a competency framework is the ideal starting-point.

Once the behavioural requirements of a job have been identified the right assessment methods must be selected. It is also important to decide who are going to act as assessors and to ensure that all such personnel are properly trained. From a practical point of view it is desirable to draw assessors from an organization's pool of HR specialists and line managers. This allows for greater organizational control and ensures that managers have a direct input into the selection process. In terms of the number of assessors required it is usual to maintain a ratio of candidates to assessors of two to one. Additionally, if the assessment centre involves a particularly broad spread of exercises, it is wise to include an extra assessor who can act as a 'master of ceremonies'. This means that a typical assessment centre for six to eight candidates will require four to five assessors.

Assessment methods

Psychometric tests and questionnaires are widely used in assessment centres. It is also standard practice to include one or two structured interviews and a number of other assessment tasks. These tasks are designed to simulate important aspects of the job and include presentations, group exercises, 'in-tray', role-play and analysis exercises. All are available 'off-the-shelf' from reputable test publishers and consultancies. However, they do require users to be appropriately trained and it is important to check your eligibility before planning an assessment centre. Alternatively, you can have exercises designed for you, but this can be an expensive process unless your organization has a long-term commitment to using this approach.

Presentations

Many assessment centres include some form of presentation exercise. These are usually structured around material which is supplied to the candidate in advance of the talk. For example, the candidate may be asked to read a case study and to present the main points or to analyse some information relating to a business problem and to articulate a solution. Whatever the task, the important elements are the provision of a number of briefing documents, the preparation of a talk by the candidate, and its subsequent delivery to an audience. Needless to say, the preparation and performance time is strictly timed: for example, a candidate may be given 30 minutes to prepare a ten-minute talk, with an extra five minutes allocated for questions.

A typical scenario might involve the candidate making a formal presentation to the 'managing director' of a company which is considering relocation. The documents provided before the talk give details on the relative merits of three different locations. The task is to evaluate the three options and to make a persuasive case for one of them.

The aspects of communication which are typically rated include:

- **Content:** Is there a clear introduction? Is information presented in a logical sequence?
- **Argument:** Are arguments easy to follow? Is the candidate's case convincing?
- **Delivery:** Does the candidate speak clearly? Is the presentation well paced?

When conducted formally a presentation is a useful way of assessing oral communication ability. It can also provide valuable information on attention to detail, problem analysis, judgement, decisiveness and personal impact, the latter including aspects of persuasiveness and performance under pressure.

Group exercises

There are many different forms of group exercise which can be used in assessment centres, all of which involve candidates debating a given topic or working on a specific problem. The important point is to carefully assess and monitor each candidate's contribution. For example, in 'leaderless discussion groups' candidates are all given the same brief and asked to discuss a particular business issue, or debate a controversial topic such as nuclear energy or Third World debt. As the discussion is 'leaderless' the aim is to discover how candidates organize the discussion and interact with each other. Thus assessors monitor the nature and pattern of each candidate's contribution. To make the rating process objective assessors rate against a fixed set of categories. For example, behaviour can be broken down into questioning, suggesting, supporting, summarizing and so forth.

Assessors will also be concerned with whether one candidate actually does take the lead, and the overall level of someone's contribution. For instance, does a particular candidate remain relatively quiet and then make an important contribution towards the end of the discussion?

Leaderless group discussions usually take about an hour to complete and are used to gather information on oral communication, listening, persuasiveness, teamwork, initiative and flexibility. Depending on the brief they can also be used to rate a candidate's analytic and problem-solving skills.

More complex group discussions are based on assigned roles and a problem scenario in which group members have competing interests. Candidates may, for instance, be asked to assume different functional roles and make the case for their particular 'department'. The briefing documents include general information and details which are specific to the role each candidate is playing. Thus candidates may act as the managers in the marketing, production, finance and R & D departments and have to negotiate for the preferential allocation of resources. In addition, candidates may also have to ensure that whatever decisions are made are in the best interests of the company as a whole.

It is interesting to note that in assigned role group discussions there will always be 'winners' and 'losers'. However, this is often not the critical factor as assessors are more concerned with the structure and quality of the arguments presented. Indeed, in some scenarios candidates receive extra credit for realizing that they should be supporting the case of another candidate, rather than distorting the allocation of available resources.

Assigned role group discussions are more structured than leaderless discussions, with specific times allocated for preparation and discussion – say, 30 minutes to read the briefing documents and prepare a case, and 60 minutes for the discussion itself. Within the discussion each candidate may be allocated a fixed time – perhaps ten minutes – to present without interruption. This type of format is used to assess candidates' communication and persuasiveness skills, as well as such attributes as interpersonal sensitivity and organizational ability.

In-tray exercises

The in-tray exercise is designed to assess the administrative aspects of a job. The task is to manage an in-tray containing between 20 and 30 items which is typical of the workload in the target job. Thus the in-tray contains various forms of information – letters, faxes, reports, e-mails and so on – which must be actioned in a fixed period of time. Documents relating to the structure of the organization, such as an organization chart, may also be included so that decisions can be made on delegating some of the tasks.

The main task is to sort through all the material, produce a list of what needs to be done in order of priority; and then action each item. This may involve writing a memo, letter or fax to a named person, deciding to make a telephone call (and indicating what would be said), or delegating to a subordinate member of staff. Sometimes, as the in-tray exercise progresses, actioned items are collected and new items are delivered, forcing the candidate to reprioritize all the items remaining in the in-tray.

A typical scenario is that the candidate has been away from the office for some time and has returned to take over a new position. The previous incumbent has left the organization and cannot be contacted. The candidate has two hours to clear the in-tray before an important meeting. At the meeting the candidate will be asked to explain how a number of projects, based on items in the in-tray, are progressing.

This type of exercise provides information on aspects of written communication, planning, problem analysis, judgement and delegation. If it is combined with an interview in which the candidate is asked to explain why, for example, certain items were not dealt with, it can also be used to assess oral communication, independence and initiative.

Other exercises

Assessment centres often include role-play exercises which are designed to simulate the interpersonal aspects of a job, a classic example being dealing with an actor (or trained manager) playing the part of an angry and dissatisfied customer. When conducted under controlled conditions such exercises are good ways of assessing customer service, listening and interpersonal sensitivity competencies. Other scenarios requiring candidates to deal with 'subordinates' can provide information on management control and leadership abilities.

Finally, in many selection situations, analysis exercises are used. These require the candidate to analyse various sorts of data, both quantitative and qualitative, in order to produce a written report with strategic recommendations. For example, the candidate may be provided with a range of information on products, customers and markets and be asked to develop a marketing strategy. In some assessment centres this task is integrated with a presentation at which the candidate has to present his or her case.

Analysis exercises generate information on a candidate's written communication, planning, detail consciousness, judgement and decisiveness. In addition, commercial awareness and numerical ability can often be assessed, as well as verbal skills and stress tolerance.

The assessment centre matrix and timetable

Tests, interviews and assessment centre exercises need to be matched against the competencies required for a job. This is done by constructing a matrix of competencies against assessment methods and by ensuring that each competency is assessed by at least two methods. Obviously, information on an individual competency may be provided by a number of methods, but some will be better than others. For example, while individual problem-solving can be assessed through interviews and group exercises, analysis and in-tray exercises will provide better information. As a result, assessment centre designers indicate how much 'weight' can be given to the results from each exercise. This allows information to be collated objectively and prevents too much attention being given to exercises which may be relatively poor indicators. An example matrix is presented in Table 3.3.

Another important requirement is a fully detailed timetable for all the assessors and candidates. The assessors need to know the timing and location of each exercise and which candidates they will be observing. Likewise, the candidates must have a clear idea of what they are doing, where and when. A master timetable for a two-day graduate assessment centre is given below in Figure 3.1.

As illustrated in the figure, the assessment centre starts with a group exercise as this provides a good 'warm-up' task for the candidates. It then moves into a period of psychometric testing, research having shown that candidates produce their best test performances when such assessments are placed at the beginning of a programme. After lunch the analysis exercise is 'buffered' with a personality questionnaire, once again to encourage peak performance as it gives the candidates an opportunity to re-acclimatize to the assessment process. The presentations and analytic exercise are delivered in two blocks so that the assessors have time to finalize ratings on the group exercise and to score and interpret the morning's tests.

Table 3.3   Assessment centre matrix

Competencies	Structured interview	Individual presentation	Analysis exercise	Personality questionnaires	Reasoning tests	In-tray exercise	Assigned role group task
				Measures			
Oral communication	■	■					■
Written communication			■			■	
Numerical analysis			■		■	▲	
Problem-solving	▲	▲	■		▲	■	▲
Planning and organizing	▲	▲	▲	▲		■	▲
Judgement	▲	▲	■	▲	▲	■	▲
Teamworking	▲	▲		▲			▲
Flexibility	▲			▲		■	■
Energy and motivation	▲	■		▲		■	■
Commercial awareness	■	▲	■		▲	▲	▲

■ Assessment method is a primary source of behavioural information.
▲ Assessment method provides valuable background information.

Day 1

10.00–10.30	Arrive & coffee (1–6; A–D)
10.30–10.45	Introduction (1–6; A–D)
10.45–12.15	Assigned role group exercise (1–6; B–D)
12.15–13.15	Verbal and numerical tests (1–6; A)
13.15–14.00	Lunch (1–6; A–D)
14.00–14.45	Personality questionnaire (1–6; B)
14.45–16.15	Individual presentations (1–3; A–C)
	Analysis exercise (4–6; D)
16.15–16.30	Tea (1–6; A–D)
16.30–18.00	Individual presentations (4–6; B–D)
	Analysis exercise (1–3; A)

Day 2

09.30–11.30	In-tray exercise (1–6; A–D)
11.30–11.40	Coffee (1–6; A–D)
11.40–12.20	Interviews (1–3; A–C)
12.20–13.00	Interviews (4–6; B–D)
13.00–14.00	Lunch (1–6; A–D)
14.00–14.15	De-brief (1–6; A–D)
14.15–15.00	Candidates depart
15.00–17.00	Assessors collate ratings (A–D)
17.00–19.00	Assessors' meeting (A–D)

Six candidates = 1–6
Four assessors = A–D

Figure 3.1   Assessment centre timetable

On the second day the candidates complete the in-tray exercise in the morning and are then interviewed in two blocks. As before, activities are deliberately ordered in this way because the in-tray exercise requires a great deal of mental effort. After lunch the candidates are formally debriefed and told what will happen next. This usually involves a brief description of how the assessors are going to reach their conclusions and when candidates will know whether or not they have been successful.

At the end of the assessment centre the assessors collect all the information they have on each candidate and complete any individual ratings. As indicated in the descriptions of some of the exercises the ratings are made against fixed categories so that the results from each candidate are directly comparable one with another. The process is, by necessity, slow and detailed and involves a number of special collation techniques. Readers who wish to explore these issues further are referred to one of the handbooks suggested in the 'Further Information' section at the end of this chapter.

Assessment centre checklist

Preparing for the assessment centre:

- Compile a detailed person specification.
- Produce a list of key competencies.
- Define competencies in behavioural terms.
- Identify a range of suitable assessment methods.
- Check the availability of exercises.
- Produce an assessment centre matrix.
- Ensure that you are properly trained.
- Make sure that other assessors are trained.
- Produce a detailed master timetable.
- Produce individual timetables for all participants.
- Secure a suitable assessment centre location.
- Organize a thorough 'dress-rehearsal'.

During the assessment centre:

- Make sure that the assessors know the timetable.
- Issue the candidates with individual timetables.
- Adhere to the timings as closely as possible.
- Ensure that the assessors record information as they go.
- Prevent ratings being discussed before the final meeting.
- Log any (unusual) events that could affect candidate performance.

After the assessment centre:

- Collate all the information on each candidate.
- Assess each candidate exercise by exercise.
- Resolve disagreements using observed evidence.
- Make final decisions on a consensual basis.
- Review the assessment centre and consider any improvements.
- Retain all candidate information for monitoring purposes.

Using psychometric techniques

Users of psychometric tests and questionnaires must be properly trained. The same applies to the exercises which are incorporated in many assessment centres. Indeed, training is even more important in this context as these are often more complicated to administer and interpret than standard tests and questionnaires. For these reasons assessment centre exercises are often delivered by business psychologists or specially trained HR personnel. To reiterate what was said earlier, those with no background in psychology or psychometric assessment will require, as a minimum, the equivalent of five days' training and if personality questionnaires are used, an additional five days' advanced instruction. Yet more training will be required for access to assessment centre materials in order to ensure that psychometric measures are used in a fair and ethical manner; employers should be extremely circumspect about purchasing materials from organizations which require no training, or which only insist on one- or two-day 'familiarization' courses.

Users need to be wary of using any form of psychometric assessment without conducting a proper job analysis, or without monitoring the effects of tests on selection decisions. Employers may well be open to legal challenge if they do not ensure that assessments are directly and unambiguously related to the job in question, and that the results of personality questionnaires, in particular, are not used in isolation. Questionnaires do not produce 'pass–fail' type results, and there is compelling evidence that men and women, for example, show significant differences in the ways in which they respond to certain types of question – particularly those relating to dominance, control and social responsibility. This makes it all too easy to indirectly discriminate between genders or, for that matter, between minority groups.

The message is clear: employers who do not monitor the effects of psychometric procedures on selection decisions do not know whether adverse impact is occurring and, consequently, leave themselves open to claims of discrimination. Nevertheless, when used appropriately psychometric assessments are one of the best ways of ensuring equal treatment of candidates because they make sure that fairness goes hand-in-hand with effectiveness.

Example OPQ® narrative report*

Occupational Personality Questionnaire Expert System

Automated Narrative Report

Concept 4.2

Mr Robert Fraser

- 11-Jun-97 -

Introduction

Mr Fraser has completed a self-report questionnaire. The questionnaire invited him to describe his behaviour, preferences and attitudes, in relation to different aspects of his working life. It is important to recognise that the answers given here are Mr Fraser's own view, and represent the way he sees his behaviour, rather than how his behaviour might be described by another person. This self-report can nevertheless give important clues to understanding Mr Fraser's perception of things and is likely to enable us to predict a good deal about his behaviour in different situations. The particular version of the questionnaire completed by Mr Fraser required him to make comparative judgements about his behaviour with an element of 'forced choice'. The profile we get from his responses highlights his perceived preferences in typical situations. This report describes Mr Fraser's profile and makes links between the various aspects involved.

Many of the comments made are to a certain extent speculative, and should be understood as hypotheses for further probing or discussion, rather than as definitive pronouncements. His responses to the questionnaire have been compared against the norm group: Professional & Managerial (1994).

Relationships with People

He seems to see himself as a leader. He tends to take charge of other people, but he also very much enjoys exercising his powers of persuasion in support of this, to carry others with him. Not only is he thus very influential, but he adds to this by holding rather strong opinions, so that he will come across as a forceful person, even to the extent of being difficult to manage. He has quite a high need for personal autonomy, although he is also reasonably able to develop a sense of identity with the group or organisation, and will not work in too isolated a way.

This marked degree of assertiveness is associated with a reasonable inclination to consult others, but in a situation of conflict he is likely to make the decisions himself. While he describes himself as having a reasonable sense of the goals towards which influences should be exerted, he might perhaps appear quite a lot more concerned with winning and with achieving a position of power. He will tend to interpret any managerial role quite flexibly, and will supervise people loosely, perhaps failing at times to follow up enough on detail. Not only does he tend to be a very prominent person, but he is also attracted to group situations and his manner of influencing people has a breadth and warmth about it.

He is quite an outgoing and fun-loving person. He also quite likes being with people, and is likely to be fairly popular. Although he may perhaps not be really interested in developing deep or intense relationships, he nevertheless likes to behave in a tactful and harmonious way. People are likely to find him quite fun to be with, but perhaps also rather unpredictable, perhaps apt to forget commitments or to disregard some social niceties.

He comes across as a socially prominent person. Not only does he seem to be naturally quite sociable, but he has also developed a good deal of confidence and polish to cope well with a range of social situations. He may seem virtually never short of the right phrase to make people feel comfortable. Whilst this social style may usually be perceived as an asset, at times it could seem to be a veneer, or he may flatter others too much for his own good.

Positive though his orientation towards people appears, it may also be tinged with a fair degree of self-interest. Thus his relationships could at times seem pragmatic, or his manner a little given to behaving in a political or diplomatic way. Whilst he will probably strike others as having a very high social profile and a commanding presence, he can seem just a little cautious about turning words into action.

Mr Fraser has a very high need for recognition of his achievements, and often likes to be in a position to compare favourably with his competitors or colleagues. He rather likes to make his mark, but not necessarily according to conventional criteria, and he perhaps even likes to accentuate his separateness from most people. His relative preoccupation with his own status and achievements is further accentuated by what might come across as a lack of interest in the feelings and needs of other people.

He may sometimes appear inconsiderate. He may not give people enough opportunity to seek his own help, and when they do he may still seem disinterested in the personal difficulties of others. His own relative lack of vulnerability to emotional problems may of course make it very difficult for him fully to empathise with the plight of people in need, or to respond with too much sensitivity to them. Although not seeming to be ready to listen to others or be tolerant of them, he can be a keen and critical judge of inter-personal issues. Whilst these perceptions may be accurate, his expression of them might appear to lack sympathy at times.

Thinking Style

Mr Fraser looks to have a predominantly abstract thinking style. His rather adventurous and open mind tends to avoid the structure and discipline needed for a rounded intellectual contribution. His ideas appear rather broad-brush, and he may need a good deal of administrative support in order to be fully effective. He is quite well attuned to psychology and the people angle of any situation, but he may be relatively less comfortable with hard data or numbers. This potential imbalance may make him subjective in his judgement, perhaps prone to over emphasis of human factors beyond the limits implied by cost and other considerations. He has a reasonable interest in visual presentation and in the appreciation of the arts, but seems less concerned about practical aspects, or about understanding how things work.

Mr Fraser likes a fair amount of change and novelty in his life, while his values tend to middle of the road, neither particularly conservative nor radical. He is quite resilient as well as being moderately adaptable, neither someone who resists change nor one who craves it for its own sake. Although he is reasonably amenable to change, his rather dominant style may make him less open to novel ideas which emanate from others, but still quite an effective change agent himself.

Although quite interested in theory and intellectual challenge, he rather prefers to avoid the sharp, critical approach which may be needed to ensure a penetrating grasp. He may therefore talk in a general, unfocussed way or take idealistic approaches on board.

His responses suggest a person who is a good generator of ideas and ingenious solutions. Allied to his conceptual approach, this should make him an imaginative innovator. He has a good level of creativity, but he tends to be an ideas person very much more than the solver of everyday practical problems. Given his balanced attitude to change, this degree of creativity may manifest itself more as evolution than revolution, modifications and variations on a theme rather than a stroke of genius. His imaginative style is supported by a reasonable degree of purposefulness, so that he should be capable of contributing quite well to strategic decisions. As well as having ideas, he has a great deal of flair in convincing other people of their value. This is allied to a strong will, which can empower his ideas and turn them into policies, but could at times imply strong belief in a somewhat dogmatic approach.

Mr Fraser seems to believe in a very structured method of operating. He does not much like the constraints of pre-determined plans, and he may distinctly prefer to think on his feet. He very much dislikes attentiveness to detail, and tends to find fixed deadlines and bureaucracy irksome. This relatively low interest in planning and preparation may mean that a lot of his marked energy to achieve results will be wasted through pursuit of too many goals, without clear priorities. Although he prefers to work without the constraints of a formal plan, he is less flexible in terms of allowing others to influence the direction of his effort, or to get him to reconsider his priorities.

His definite dislike of detail or routine may be related to his orientation towards the broad perspective. Although he tends to appear disorganised, this may be partly counteracted in terms of his wider view. Not only is he unconcerned with detail, in his approach to problems, but he is also inclined to be rather unquestioning in his thinking. Not only does he seem to find minutiae irksome, but he also seems distinctly unconcerned about them, and may well be inaccurate in his work. Although not very literal in his adherence to schedules, he has a facility for responding to time pressures.

Feelings and Emotions

Mr Fraser's responses suggest an effectively dynamic pattern. He combines a very high level of drive and focused concern counter-balanced by a marked self-assurance and control.

He is someone who very rarely experiences anxiety. Not only does he find it easy to switch off from things, but he is also able to take quite severe challenges in his stride. He has a reasonable ability to reduce tension by communicating his own marked freedom of anxiety to others. His distinctly carefree approach also has a rather 'laid-back' character, a relative lack of urgency about it. His perhaps overly positive and extremely carefree disposition could even make him blind to the possibility of failure.

He is fairly difficult to upset. He does not easily take offence, and in any case he is likely to be restrained in showing whatever emotions he is experiencing. His marked resilience and low level of tension combine to make him a comfortably adjusted person from an emotional point of view. His strong sense of assurance is associated with a considerable amount of interpersonal impact, enabling him to project himself as someone with a very clear self confidence. He seems to be someone who does not have a particularly sensitive disposition. He can put up with a fair amount of rough and tumble, and may be less concerned with matters of feelings.

His attitude to life is very much characterised by optimism and cheerfulness, but at the same time he is reasonably critical and is unlikely to take things too much at face value. His high degree of optimism is linked with a way of seeing things which is more imaginative (sometimes even extravagant) than common place. He has a reasonably communicative brand of cheerfulness, so that his considerable positiveness is fairly visible and can be a source of comfort to others. His fairly cheerful acceptance has an unchallenging, generalised quality, since he is not an attentive listener.

He is someone who sets his sights extremely high, and has a very high determination to succeed against any opposition. He will compete keenly to achieve his aims. Although not attracted to challenges relating to physical endurance per se, he sees himself as extremely motivated with respect to his career. He tends to see his aspirations in terms of his position or status, but his freedom from anxiety helps him to avoid seeming uptight about them or overly striving. He is likely to behave in a very opportunistic way, seizing chances as they come rather than planning his career in any detail. His ideas of what he wants from his working life may also be less than clear, or perhaps somewhat personal rather than conformist.

He is a person who typically responds quickly and very spontaneously to a situation, perhaps sometimes without due reflection. He is capable of making really courageous and positive decisions, with little reluctance to work at speed. He may even lack a due sense of danger on occasion. His decisions are also likely to be clear-cut ones, and carried through with distinct single-mindedness, even against considerable opposition.

Further information

Hay, J. (1997), *The Gower Assessment and Development Centre*, Aldershot: Gower.

Jackson, C. (1996), *Understanding Psychological Testing*, Leicester: BPS Books.

Jansen, P. and de Jongh, F. (1997), *Assessment Centres: A Practical Handbook*, Chichester: John Wiley.

Parkinson, M. (1997), *How to Master Psychometric Tests*, London: Kogan Page.

Woodruffe, C. (1993), *Assessment Centres: Identifying and Developing Competence*, London: IPD.

Motivation and Performance Appraisal

Overview

Once the recruitment and selection cycle is complete the organization's concern is with obtaining the best possible performance from its new recruits. This centres on the issue of motivation, or having an understanding of the psychological factors which make people work effectively. A number of surveys have shown that well motivated and contented employees work for organizations longer and are more productive and also that businesses which manage the motivational process, and actively make their staff feel valued, can increase their profits by as much as a quarter. The factors which drive this increase in performance are reviewed in this chapter, along with the techniques required to assess the different sources of motivation. The related topic of why people leave employment is also explored and illustrated with a discussion of the problems of graduate retention. However, as with many problems in business psychology, constructive interventions require an objective measurement of performance. As a result, the requirements for effective appraisal interviews, and the role of 360-degree feedback methods, are considered in some detail. Finally the important issue of job evaluation and reward management is addressed with particular reference to linking pay to competency frameworks.

What makes people work (harder)?

At a superficial level there are some self-evident answers to this question, the first being that work provides a convenient way of earning money and of maintaining a given standard of living. However, this is not the only reason why people work, as is obvious from the way in which we talk about it. A person's job is a status indicator and provides an important sense of identity. This is apparent from the fact that the first question that is often asked of a stranger is 'What do you do?'. We also have a lifelong interest in securing a job title which we feel reflects our true worth. Needless to say, this points to the importance of work in giving us a sense of achievement and purpose, and allowing us to 'master' a set of activities which society recognizes as being worthy. Additionally, work gives structure to our day and fulfils a powerful social function. This last point should not be underestimated as it has a crucial role to play both in team behaviour and in the development of other forms of work-based relationships. Incidentally, work is also a prime mover in the formation of non-work relationships with as many as 50 per cent of couples meeting their partner through work!

Yet, important as these factors are to individuals, what does actually make people work harder? This is a difficult question to answer, and the solution is not merely a matter of providing more money or a greater sense of involvement. To complicate the issue even further, key motivators probably differ between jobs, and also between people. Nevertheless there are two groups of job features which are said to promote greater job involvement, and consequently enhanced performance. These features, first identified through a study of sales professionals in the USA, form two motivational clusters, 'psychological safety' and 'job meaningfulness':

■ **Psychological safety**
  - **Support.** Workers are given authority to make their own decisions. The decisions they make are supported by their immediate superiors.
  - **Role clarity.** Workers know exactly what is expected of them. The way in which their work is assessed, and the standard of work required, is made explicit.
  - **Recognition.** Workers, or employees working in teams, receive credit and appropriate praise for their contribution.
■ **Job meaningfulness**
  - **Self-expression.** Workers are encouraged to develop their own style of working and to feel able to express their own personalities.
  - **Contribution.** Workers should not feel like a 'small cog in a large machine' and must be able to see that their effort makes a difference.
  - **Challenge.** Workers should experience work as a source of positive stimulation. Individual tasks should stretch people's abilities.

In a sales context two of these features were particularly influential in making people work harder. These were self-expression and the promotion of the feeling that new ideas were welcome, and the perception that the organization recognized and appreciated the significance of the sales role. Many of the other features were important, but not as motivating, and crucially target-setting was not seen as a prime motivator. The latter is a striking result when one considers the way in which most sales organizations operate.

To summarize, job meaningfulness and psychological safety combine to generate job involvement. This in turn makes it more likely that people will commit more time and energy to work leading to a better quality of performance. It has been observed that job involvement is similar to love in that highly job-involved people are focused on work to the exclusion of practically everything else. Work becomes the purpose of their lives and they are often willing to work as many hours as it takes to finish a job because they genuinely enjoy what they are doing. Whether or not this level of activity is healthy is a different question, but the ultimate aim of an organization is to increase its employees' feelings of job involvement. An additional consideration which becomes apparent from what has been said so far is that job involvement is a function of the sort of features described and cannot be induced by getting people to work more intensely or to stay at work longer. This is another illuminating result in that many employers believe that improvement in performance merely means obtaining more physical or mental effort from their employees. The issue is clearly rather more complicated than this, and crude measures of input, such as length of working time, do not equate to quality of performance. This has all sorts of implications, not least to arguments over maximum working hours, annual hour contracts, flexitime and so on.

For those interested in the differences between occupational groups, recent research by Oxford Psychologists Press reveals that the prime motivation for HR professionals is job meaningfulness. They need to feel that they are an integral part of an organization and that they are making an important contribution to its functioning. In these circumstances they are prepared to commit time and effort, which in turn reinforces the view that they are working in an environment which is supportive and encourages self-expression. This is the reverse of what happens with salespeople – they need to feel that they can express themselves before they invest more effort. Of course, the corollary is that with HR people the provision of opportunities for greater self-expression is not likely to lead to greater job involvement! This finding has important implications for motivating this particular group of workers. No doubt similar differences operate with other groups, and it is subtleties such as these which need to be identified if we are to be able to quantify the influences on someone's motivation to work.

Measuring motivation

One of the most popular ways of measuring the effects of different sources of motivation on an individual is to use a self-report questionnaire. Such questionnaires are similar in construction to those used to measure personality but concentrate on dimensions which are specific to work motivation. For example the *Motivation Questionnaire* (MQ), designed by the UK test publisher Saville & Holsworth Ltd, measures four principal dimensions of motivation: 'energy and dynamism', 'synergy', and 'intrinsic' and 'extrinsic' factors. These dimensions are described fully in the example at the end of this chapter (pp 97–8), but, essentially, energy and dynamism concern such factors as the need for achievement and competition, synergy aspects of motivation such as recognition and personal growth, intrinsic individual needs such as work flexibility and autonomy, and extrinsic traditional motivators like money and status.

The MQ presents respondents with 144 employment situations and asks them to rate the effect that each would have on their motivation to work. In all, it measures 18 different aspects of motivation providing a comprehensive profile of a person's 'motivational style'. In practice the profile is presented as a chart, accompanied by a number of tables and explanatory text. An extract from a report produced for a fictional candidate called 'Julie Ross' is presented in Table 4.1.

Table 4.1   Example motivation narrative

Situations with considerable impact on Ms Julie Ross's motivation

Motivators	Demotivators
Working under pressure at a fast pace	Leisurely pace of work, no deadlines
Challenging targets, overcoming difficulties	Moderate objectives, undemanding work
Competition	Little opportunity to compare her performance with that of others
Influence, authority, power	Lack of responsibility, no input in decision-making
Meeting people, teamwork, helping others	Absent or poor relations with others
Secure and pleasant conditions	Job insecurity or discomfort conditions
Scope for personal growth	Few opportunities to learn
Stimulating and varied or creative work	Routine or uninteresting work

As with all self-report measures, the validity of the results depend on the self-insight and honesty of the person completing the questionnaire. However, when completed in a realistic way, the results can provide a useful background to staff development, counselling and performance management activities. The use of a questionnaire also allows employers to keep track of the changes in an employee's perception of work and to match these with new challenges and opportunities. This can be of great importance in situations such as graduate development as it helps maximize individual effort and prevent loss of potential.

The MQ is only one example of a motivation questionnaire, and a number of other publishers produce similar products. Other UK examples are *Motive-A* published by the Test Agency Ltd, the *Motivation and Culture Fit Questionnaire* from the Criterion Partnership and the *Motivation Fit System* from Development Dimensions International Ltd. Contact details are provided at the end of this book. However, readers are reminded that access to questionnaires such as these is restricted to those with appropriate training. In the UK this implies at least the successful completion of a British Psychological Society Level-B course – see Chapter 3, p. 62 for further information.

Case study: motivating call-centre operators

Over recent years telemarketing and telesales activities have increased dramatically. Centralized 'call-centres' now offer a vast range of sales and marketing services, as well as providing up-to-date consumer information on services like travel and health. Across the EU call-centres provide employment for one in 250 of the working population. Even more dramatic is the figure in the UK, the European market leader in this area, in which numbers are rapidly approaching one in 100. However, call-centres require a particular type of employee, and many organizations are facing significant problems in retaining skilled operators.

The growth in the call-centre market has been dominated by the financial services industry. One such organization found that it was losing up to a half of its staff on an annual basis, at a replacement cost per operator of over £4500. This high 'burn-out' rate was mirrored by declining levels of job satisfaction, with one internal survey suggesting that work satisfaction declined by at least a third every 12 months. As the success of 'direct' sales operations is directly linked to the commitment and motivation of the staff the organization recognized this as a serious problem.

The organization decided to tackle the problem by reviewing its selection strategy and management practices. The person specification for call-centre operators focused on well developed communication skills, being responsive, methodical, reliable and considerate, and on having an open and extroverted manner. Once recruited, operators were given product training and were subject to tight control through the use of an automated call distribution system (ACD). ACDs remove the need for a switchboard and allow managers to monitor the length of calls and completion times; many also track operator 'success' by calculating the ratio of sales to calls.

Employee research revealed that those who were highly extroverted were good performers, but were more likely to become bored and leave. Surprisingly, being excessively organized and methodical also led to lower performance, perhaps because it stopped operators making a sufficient number of calls per day. The operators also commented that the level of control over their work put them under considerable stress and reduced their job satisfaction; in addition, the use of a script which told them what to say to callers made them feel little more than robots.

As a result of the research and consultation with its employees the organization decided to change its selection policy. This involved actively recruiting those who were less extroverted, slightly less organized and more flexible. In parallel, a number of changes were made to the working environment which involved giving operators a greater say in how work was distributed through the use of self-managed teams. Operators were also retrained so that they could handle a greater variety of calls and given discretion to 'modify' their scripts as appropriate. Finally, managers were encouraged to act more as 'coaches' and to become actively involved in developing staff, rather than merely monitoring sales data.

A follow-up survey showed that operators' (and managers') motivation levels had increased significantly, and that the high turnover rate was attributable to recruitment and management, rather than 'burn-out'. The changes also had a marked effect on retention and reduced the leaver rate to 20 per cent per annum.

The problems of graduate retention

Many organizations face a problem in retaining their key managers – an issue which is of particular importance when it comes to graduate and professional staff, not only because they cost more to recruit and employ, but also because they represent a strategic resource and much of the organization's intellectual capital. Intellectual capital is of prime importance to technological firms, or in any organization which faces intense competition, because its loss can lead to sensitive information being passed to competitors. This is a real danger with young graduates as, at the beginning of their careers, they tend to change jobs every two years or so.

Graduates are often attracted to jobs because of the status of an organization (especially if it is a 'big name'), by its location, and by opportunities for future training and development. Unfortunately few organizations live up to their own publicity and many graduates become rapidly disillusioned. This is a dangerous time and the enlightened employer is well advised to develop strategies which identify the causes of dissatisfaction, and to provide a range of suitable remedies. In the UK a large body of evidence reveals that the principal causes of low morale are:

- lack of challenge and the feeling that abilities are not being used
- little attention from superiors, and, at best, patchy 'mentoring'
- poor performance appraisal and career management
- reduced opportunities for training once initial schemes have been completed
- organizational politics and office infighting.

In short, young graduates are often left to fend for themselves and to manage their own careers, while being restrained by work pressures and a lack of guidance. In response employers often react by offering dissatisfied 'high-flyers' more money – a one-shot strategy that seldom works. Indeed, evidence from a number of surveys reveals that only 10 per cent of employees say that remuneration is the main reason for leaving a job. Many of the factors mentioned previously, such as a lack of opportunity to use and develop skills, are rated higher. From an organizational point of view it should also be recognized that 'loyalty' bonuses distort reward systems and lead to resentment among other employees. A better approach is to identify those employees you wish to retain, discover the factors which cause them to leave (or stay), and develop an effective retention strategy.

The first part requires a risk analysis. This is a two-stage process which concentrates on identifying high-risk groups and the effects of losing particular employees. For example, young well qualified graduates with marketable skills are an obvious high-risk group, particularly as they often have few domestic or personal ties and have the energy to look for alternative positions. However, the problem is not just restricted to graduates; any employee who possesses skills which are in demand in the employment market must be classified as high-risk. Furthermore, if the loss of any of these employees is likely to lead to problems in performing the organization's core work then the consequences can be severe.

Once high-risk groups have been isolated the task is to find out why people are leaving. This can be a result of a combination of any of the factors described in this chapter so far, but the trick is to discover which are the most influential. One way of doing this is to conduct regular satisfaction surveys coupled with focus groups, or to use carefully planned 'exit' interviews. Exit interviews can be particularly effective as they involve asking departing employees, who now have little to lose, for their reasons for leaving. As such, they can provide a quality and honesty of information that is difficult to obtain in any other way.

Finally, information received must be acted on, and a responsive retention strategy put in place. This is unlikely to involve the manipulation of just one aspect of the employment equation, but rather the management of a series of interdependent factors. A well conducted risk analysis will also allow an organization to target its efforts on those groups who are genuinely important to its long-term prospects. In practice the most effective interventions are found to involve:

- **Focused selection.** A well conducted job analysis linked to objective selection techniques allows candidates to be closely matched with jobs. Recruitment information should convey a realistic image of the organization and not lead to expectations which cannot be fulfilled. For instance, advertisements should not suggest that rapid progress is possible unless there is a realistic chance of promotion.
- **Tailored training.** Training programmes must be in place before new staff are recruited. They should be tailored to individual needs and take account of the recruit's psychological profile. For example, extroverts need to be continually active and respond best to activity-based learning, whereas introverts often prefer to absorb information at their own speed from manuals and other written sources.
- **Responsive management.** Managers need to adapt their style to promote team spirit and individual development. They should be trained in mentoring and coaching skills and work to a set of clear guidelines. Managers must take an active interest in staff training, ensure that training targets are set and met, and provide careers guidance at the end of any formal training period.
- **Enriched job content.** Jobs should include elements of individual and teamwork. Teamwork should be especially encouraged as most businesses rely on the coordinated work of a number of people. Allowing team members to organize the distribution of work within the team is also found to produce a more effective use of human resources.
- **Autonomous working.** Wherever possible, employees should be given flexibility with regard to where they work and their working hours. Quality of output is not just a simple question of working longer hours, or working at particular periods during the day, but to working intelligently within the parameters of the business.
- **Equitable reward systems.** Pay should be linked to individual or team output and not to the risk of losing particular employees. Loyalty bonuses only offer a short-term fix and, as has been suggested, do not necessarily mean that employees will stay in post.

Motivation and retention checklist

- Identify key employee groups within the organization.
- Conduct a structured risk analysis.

- Gather quantifiable information using questionnaires, surveys and exit interviews.
- Establish the causes of employee satisfaction/dissatisfaction.
- Act to modify selection and assessment processes, if appropriate.
- Develop a strategy for promoting greater motivation and improved retention.
- Train managers to deliver and monitor the new strategy.
- Use a combination of training, work pattern and job content approaches.
- Avoid the crude manipulation of pay scales or the use of loyalty bonuses.
- Review changes and monitor the effects on staff motivation and retention rates.

Performance appraisal

Motivation and staff retention are closely related to performance appraisal. This is the process of reviewing operational objectives such as past achievements, and the setting of targets for future performance. It is also directly linked to personal objectives such as training and development. All these issues have a direct bearing on individual motivation and can lead both to increased and decreased performance. When appraisals are dealt with badly – and many organizations realize that they do not carry out appraisals effectively – they are perceived as occasions which allow for little more than the opportunity to criticize. On the other hand, when they are managed in an informed manner they can provide a positive experience for appraisers and appraisees alike, and become a powerful way of motivating staff.

Appraisal planning

An appraisal may concentrate on a number of different concerns but, whatever the objective, it should be seen as part of a continuous process of annual review between an employee and his or her manager which gives both parties an opportunity to discuss performance. The principle of the appraisal is actually very simple: it concentrates on making sure that employees know exactly what their jobs entail; how well they have to be done; and how they will know whether they have performed at the appropriate level.

The discussion usually takes the form of an interview and, like any interview, it needs to be preplanned and follow a logical sequence. It is particularly important that it is treated as a significant part of an employee's development and that sufficient time is allowed for a thorough exchange of views. The physical environment should also reflect the importance which is attached to the appraisal; it must be quiet and away from any busy work areas. The main focus should be on achievements and progress, leading to a plan of action for the forthcoming year. The emphasis on positive progress is important, as an appraisal which takes the form of a post mortem, or is weighted more towards the 'stick' than the 'carrot', will only demotivate and cause resentment towards both the appraisal and the appraiser on the part of the appraisee.

The line manager and appraisee must both prepare carefully before the interview. The manager should ensure that an up-to-date job description is available and collate individual performance information, the latter ideally being in the form of notes which have been made throughout the year. It is also important to consider the sort of objectives which need to be clarified, and how the discussion will be split between considering the needs of the organization and those of the individual. Importantly, managers must analyse the reasons why an employee has been successful or not and decide where to give praise, and how to deal with underperformance constructively. In addition, time must be spent considering the individual's operational and personal objectives for the forthcoming period. Similarly, appraisees should prepare notes which identify how they have met their objectives, both in business and personal terms, and be ready to appraise their own performance at the interview. Appraisees should also be ready to discuss any pressing issues concerning the nature of their work or their long-term prospects. Some organizations allow staff to formally prepare for appraisals and to complete their own comprehensive self-appraisal questionnaire which then forms the basis of the discussion.

Conducting an appraisal

The skills required for appraisal interviewing are similar to those used in selection. This means that the manager should use open-ended questions and allow the appraisee to do most of the talking. This format provides plenty of 'space' for discussion and enables appraisees to air any issues that are important to them and to feel that they have had a fair hearing. The skilled manager will also ensure that the appraisee is invited to consider his or her own performance and that important matters are then analysed jointly. Crucially, the discussion must be managed so that it is based on facts and not opinions, on performance and not personality. This is achieved by referring to actual events and not to hypothetical situations. For example, using a critical incident technique (see Chapter 1), appraisees can be led through a series of questions which relate to a given situation, as follows:

- 'How did you plan project X?'
- 'Who worked with you?'
- 'How well did you work together?'
- 'What did you do?'
- 'What was the outcome?'
- 'Why were you successful/unsuccessful?'
- 'What did you learn about yourself?'
- 'What would you do differently in the future?'

Of course, if a line manager is conducting the appraisal the answers to some of these questions will be known, but the point is to discover how the appraisee perceives events. In those situations where things did not go according to plan the manager should not criticize or attribute blame. This sort of feedback, if deserved, should have been delivered at the time. The last point leads to a useful rule which applies to all appraisals – don't deliver unexpected criticisms. The appraisal is not a time for surprises but for a rational review of progress and how it can be improved. This is best achieved by sticking to the facts, using appropriate praise, and by agreeing honest, measurable and realistic objectives. Along the way the appraisee should also be given an opening to discuss issues which the manager should consider, so that the manager can use the appraisal as a means of obtaining feedback about his or her own performance as well. Questions which address this often neglected area include:

- 'What can I do to help you achieve your objectives more easily?'
- 'Does my management style make your job more difficult?'

Conducting a thorough appraisal requires considerable time and effort. The manager must be well briefed, and not consider the activity as a chore which needs to be completed as soon as possible; the appraisee must use the discussion as an opportunity to review his or her progress and as a platform to push for extra training and development. Sometimes it is also the appropriate forum to discuss salary increases or bonuses, although this depends on the way in which the organization manages the reward process and on the link between pay and performance. Finally, it is incumbent upon all appraisers to make sure that they are properly trained. Just as there is no such thing as a natural selection interviewer, there is no such thing as a natural appraiser. Both require the effective and disciplined use of a particular set of skills if they are to yield results which support the organization's needs.

360-degree feedback

Multi-source appraisal, often called 360-degree feedback, is a relatively new technique which allows for appraisal information to be gathered from a number of different sources. These include not only the appraisee but his or her direct reports, line managers and, in some instances, customers or clients. Such feedback provides a more complete view of an individual and provides a powerful technique for identifying development needs and improving performance. The technique has also proved to be useful for initiating cultural change in organizations and in reinforcing new behaviours and core competencies.

360-degree feedback is usually carried out by using a series of 'paper-and-pencil' questionnaires, although recently a number of consultancies have begun to offer the option of information collection through the Internet. However, whatever the method of collection, the information is then collated across respondents and a comprehensive feedback report prepared. A good example is *Skillscope™*, published in the USA by the Center for Creative Leadership and distributed in the UK by Oxford Psychologists Press, which is a multi-rater-based instrument based on a 98-item questionnaire. The questions ask about 15 skill clusters which have been shown to be of particular importance in the workplace (see Table 4.2 for further details). The questionnaires are supplied in sets of ten, with one for the respondent, and up to a further nine for his or her 'appraisers'. In practice, at least six questionnaires are usually completed as this helps to ensure a comprehensive view of the respondent and appraiser confidentiality. The resulting report gives a detailed picture of the respondent's strengths and development needs and provides crucial information on their importance to the respondent's job role. In addition,

Table 4.2   Skillscope™ skill clusters

1 Getting and making sense of information
2 Communicating information and ideas
3 Taking action, making decisions
4 Risk-taking, innovation
5 Energy, drive, ambition
6 Relationships
7 Influencing, leadership, power
8 Openness to influence, flexibility
9 Administrative/organizational ability
10 Managing conflict, negotiation
11 Time management
12 Selecting, developing people
13 Knowledge of job, business
14 Coping with pressure, adversity, integrity
15 Self-management, self-insight, self-development

Skillscope™ is a trademark of the Center for Creative Leadership, Greensboro, NC 27438-6300, USA.

it is possible to combine the results from more than one respondent – for example, from a work team or group – and to produce a report which integrates appraisal information.

A number of other UK test publishers distribute similar questionnaires, notably the *Inventory of Management Competencies* and *Perspectives on Management Competencies* from Saville & Holdsworth Ltd, the *Personal Competency Framework* from ASE, and *Benchmarks™*, another questionnaire distributed by Oxford Psychologists Press. All provide 'expert' reports which can be used in all forms of appraisal and development situations. Some are also linked to development planning guides or individual workbooks. These allow for further analysis of the questionnaire results and the setting of developmental objectives.

However, a word of warning when selecting published questionnaires for use in appraisal – make sure that the 360-degree instrument is appropriate for the purpose and that you have been properly trained to use it. Also ensure that information is treated in the strictest confidence and that respondents receive feedback in line with the publisher's instructions. This obviously involves providing accurate information on the results and the confidence which can be placed in them, and also making respondents aware of their shelf-life.

While traditional 'manager–subordinate' appraisal methods are still the most popular way of conducting appraisals a greater number of businesses are now considering the use of 360-degree methods. Indeed, a recent survey by the UK-based Industrial Society indicates that only 5 per cent of managers believe that traditional methods will still be acceptable in ten years' time, and over 40 per cent that the most important additional method will be 360-degree feedback.

Case study: 360-degree feedback

A large public service organization decided to incorporate a 360-degree feedback process in its appraisal activities. This was prompted by an employee survey which suggested that organizational change was dependent on a 'new deal' between managers and their staff. The results showed that staff felt that their efforts where not sufficiently recognized or appreciated, and that the 'downwards' flow of information was often blocked by managers.

The feedback process was based on a questionnaire which was distributed to all staff. It was designed to allow the members of different work groups to assess their immediate supervisors and managers – a process of 'upward' appraisal. In a parallel operation managers were asked to complete questionnaires on the members of groups for which they had direct responsibility. After a careful introductory process, in which participants were assured of the confidentiality of their responses, over 250 employees completed questionnaires.

To reinforce the impartiality of the process the data collected was analysed using an external bureau service. Individual reports were then produced for each participant, as well as summaries which analysed the overall ratings for staff and bosses respectively. The results were fed back by specially trained facilitators in both group and individual sessions. During the individual sessions participants were encouraged to focus on areas of strength and also on those aspects of the manager–subordinate relationship in which they could improve.

The 360-degree process confirmed the view that staff perceived their managers as being aloof and poor at communicating. Individual appraisals suggested that managers needed to improve their people management skills, especially in the area of staff motivation, and that a complete overhaul of the way in which information was disseminated within the organization was also required. Likewise, managers viewed many staff as lacking in results-orientation, with a significant number being appraised as being low on energy and drive.*

A series of action plans was produced to tackle the issues which had been highlighted. These were linked to an appraisal interview-based review programme. At an organizational level it was also decided to monitor progress by using an attitude questionnaire at regular intervals.

Appraisal interview checklist

■ Use a recent and detailed job description.
■ Collate individual performance data.
■ Collect additional data, using questionnaires.
■ Remind the appraisee of the purpose of the discussion.
■ Agree the agenda with the appraisee.
■ Review the aims and actions agreed at the last appraisal.
■ Evaluate how effectively aims have been achieved.
■ Double-check performance against the job description.
■ Agree job performance aims for the next appraisal.
■ Discuss what training or development is required.
■ Agree what needs to be done, by whom and by when.
■ Provide an opportunity for any other issues to be raised.

Reward management

While pay may be a crude way of influencing individual motivation, the management of an equitable reward system is of prime importance in maintaining a healthy and dynamic organization. Such a system requires

---

* As is often the case in these situations the two sets of perceptions are linked. There is a circular relationship between lack of encouragement and lack of drive.

a business to perform formal job evaluations which are designed to discover the relative 'worth' of different jobs within the organization. From these evaluations flows a way of coordinating what, in many organizations, is a rather haphazard pay structure in such a way that rational and defensible pay decisions can be made. It is also valuable to realize that job evaluation provides a direct link between the direction of a business and the strategic value of the roles within it. For example, mission statements and organizational objectives are only achieved through people adding value to the jobs assigned to them. However, to return to the more obvious reason for job evaluation, it is to provide a meaningful frame of reference so that consistent decisions can be taken in the light of existing and realistic differentials – this is not only a question of deciding how much to pay an individual, but how this relates to what everyone else is paid.

Obviously this whole process relies on being able to attach a worth to a job. Technically this involves the identification of what is known as 'intrinsic value', or the notion that what employees are worth is related to who they are, their employment or educational background, and what they do. To do this, the following factors are often taken into account:

- **Impact**. What difference do the job-holder's activities make to the way in which business objectives are achieved?
- **Expertise**. How is the level of expertise or knowledge of the job-holder related to how well the job is done?
- **Responsibility**. What level of personal responsibility does the job-holder assume for the job being performed?
- **Competence**. In what, and to what extent, does the job-holder have to be competent to work effectively?

It would also be usual to consider the physical demands of a job in terms of the effort required to perform it, and, in some instances, any unusual mental demands made on the job-holder in terms of decisions made in stressful or pressurized situations. For instance, when evaluating the factors which bear on being a successful air traffic controller it would be important to assess the relationship between personal responsibility and the mental demands of the job. What is also apparent from considering the factors mentioned is that they do not take into account features such as the organization's culture or the 'market value' of a particular job. Thus in some organizations, such as those in the service sector, it may be traditional to reward certain groups of workers in a given way, and pay scales will often be benchmarked against those of competitors. The latter is an important point as market value significantly influences rates of pay. Indeed, in some businesses – especially those which rely on specialist workers who are on short supply – it is the principal factor in

deciding what to pay people. At an individual level it should also be realized that, even if employees perceive their pay as being fair in the context
of their parent organization, they will still be dissatisfied if it is out of line
with comparable jobs in the same industry. This, of course, makes it difficult for an employer to produce a completely objective system, especially
if the organization operates in a number of different locations throughout
a country, since, in such circumstances, employees will not only compare
their pay with local rates but with the national picture as well. This is the
classic pay dilemma, and one that is played out annually in the UK when
public service unions negotiate pay rises with the government and when
multinational companies attempt to equate pay systems across different
countries.

Evaluating jobs

The first task is to decide what sort of jobs will be evaluated. This is no
mean feat as, in some organizations, there may be up to 200 different job
titles. To complicate matters further it may also be necessary to evaluate a
number of different job-holders for each target job. In addition, the organization needs to decide if one scheme is to be applied across all jobs,
or if a number of schemes will be used. Once these issues have been
resolved, a job evaluation programme can begin. This typically involves
five stages:

1 Select target jobs.
2 Identify the basis for evaluation.
3 Analyse target jobs.
4 Evaluate jobs.
5 Design a pay structure.

The first stage is one of the most crucial as it relies on the identification of
a representative sample of jobs. This must reflect the full range of jobs
which are performed within an organization and, if desired, also allow
for direct comparisons with similar positions in competitor businesses. As
a rule of thumb, evaluators should aim to gather information on at least
three examples of each target job. The next stage involves the identification of factors which are common to all jobs, but are present in varying
degrees in different jobs. A competency framework (see Chapter 1) is useful at this stage as this will reveal many of the factors required plus information on performance levels. When a suitable range of factors have been
isolated – maybe eight or ten – the target jobs are analysed and evaluated.
The output at this stage will be a series of job descriptions which can be
used to rank one job against another, or to compare a job to some form of
predetermined scale.

Many job evaluation schemes compare whole jobs with each other and make no attempt to differentiate at a factor level. Such non-analytical approaches place jobs in a 'pecking' order by comparing successive pairs of jobs, or by comparing jobs one at a time with benchmark jobs which are assumed to be correctly graded. The aim is to develop pay rates which reflect the need for jobs of equal value to be rewarded in the same way. This is a legal requirement in the UK through the provisions of the Equal Pay Act. The alternative is to use an analytical scheme or one that relies on 'point-factor' rating. As the name implies, a point-factor approach assesses the degree to which given factors are present in a particular job and then, depending on the relative importance of each factor, assigns points. In this way, if jobs are systematically assessed on a factor-by-factor basis, each can be assigned a unique numerical value. These values can then be used to directly construct a pay scale, the only outstanding issues being how to fix the base rate or how to deal with any special interest groups.

Just like the point-factor approach, a ranking system requires a base rate to be established. However, although it is more simple to devise it has the distinct disadvantage of only being based on a simple ordering of jobs and takes no account of the differentials between them. For example, a supervisory job may be rated as more 'valuable' than a production job, but how much more valuable is it?

Job evaluation packages

The job evaluation process described not only relies on the skilled analysis and evaluation of a series of jobs, it also requires considerable effort and time to carry out effectively. Because of this, many organizations use 'off-the-shelf' evaluation packages or retain the services of a consultant who specializes in reward management issues.

One package, the *Hay Guide Chart-Profile Method*, is the most widely used job evaluation method in the world. It is used in some 40 different countries and underpins the pay schemes of over 8000 different organizations. The method is based on three key principles – namely:

- All jobs exist to provide a contribution to the organization's output.
- Job performance requires an input of knowledge, skills and experience.
- Job competence is used to solve the problems that arise in a job.

These three principles relate to the factors of 'accountability', 'know-how' and 'problem-solving' respectively. All jobs can be described using these terms: for example, 'know-how' can be broken down into technical, procedural or professional knowledge and skill; planning, organizing and managerial skills; and human relations skills. For each of the three main factors a guide, which contains a descriptive scale for each element and a numbering system, is used. The numbering system is based on a 15 per cent 'step' difference – in other words, there is a 15 per cent gap between each set of criteria for each element. At the end of the process, 'job size' is determined by combining the results of the three factors.

The job evaluation data produced by the *Chart-Profile Method* is used to develop a pay structure by making judgements about the balance of factors in all the jobs under review and by developing one of the following:

- a pay scale based on absolute job size
- a grading system based on groups of jobs of the same size
- a banding system across all jobs within the organization
- 'job families' based on jobs requiring similar skills, competencies.

In addition, because of its standardized nature and widespread use, the method allows for valid comparisons with the systems used by other similar-sized employers. This is a very powerful feature as it automatically places a client organization's remuneration system in the context of the contemporary 'pay market'. Readers may also be interested to know that the system is available as an MS Windows-based program called *HRXpert*. This provides a flexible way of generating tailor-made questionnaires which can be used to directly compare one job with another, or on a group or family basis.

Other sophisticated job evaluation packages are widely available. For example, in the UK, KPMG Management Consulting produce *Equate*; the PA Consulting Group, the *Basic Job Evaluation Scheme*; PE Consulting, the *Pay Points System*; Price Waterhouse, the *Profile Methodology*; and Saville & Holdsworth, the *Job Evaluation Method*. Contact details are available at the end of this book. Most of the firms quoted also provide services on a global basis.

Job evaluation and competencies

It has been suggested that a useful starting-point for a job evaluation system is a competency framework, since many organizations already use the competency approach, or something like it, for selection or development purposes. Also, most competency frameworks are efficient at differentiating between individuals and so are the natural starting-point for person-based pay schemes. Such schemes are probably equally as popular as job-based approaches because they allow the changing nature of a person's work to be taken into account. However, whatever the frame of reference, it must be remembered that competencies need to be carefully defined and weighted: in short, managers must decide which competencies are the most important and rank them. This is not easy to do as competencies range from those which can be developed to those which appear to be in-built. Thus, while it might be reasonable to relate pay, at least in part, to improvements in an employee's general communication and negotiation skills, is it sensible to withhold rewards because an employee is not being as innovative as expected?

The issue is further complicated by the fact that organizations usually select staff on the basis of their in-built competencies as these are generally easier to assess. However, the dilemma is that such competencies may not carry the same competitive advantage as those which require time and effort to develop. The wise employer might therefore be better advised to stimulate potential through a more flexible approach to competencies and pay, rather than to merely reward those competencies which an employee had before recruitment. Yet, in a rapidly changing world of work, it is difficult to know what is 'the right stuff'. To this problem psychology has three possible solutions:

- Give more weight to competencies which require change orientation, flexibility and mental agility. This should ensure that employees learn and develop quicker and do not just mirror the competency profile of the existing workforce.
- Take account of 'conceptual' competencies, particularly those which have been shown to be related to superior performance – for example, 'strategic' competencies or those which are related to 'future forecasting' predict performance.
- Create a fluid link between competencies and pay which recognizes that some competencies have an identifiable life cycle. Thus some competencies may be important for present performance but are likely to be less useful in the future, whereas others may be 'emerging'. An example of an emerging competency would be the ability to work as part of a 'virtual' team (see Chapter 5).

In summary it is important to do your homework and to identify person or job characteristics which are linked to performance. Furthermore, you should view such attributes as the inputs into a process which needs to reward superior performance while also recognizing that there are other factors which are of equal importance – namely, the opportunity for individuals to develop and refine competencies which meet the organization's future needs. It is in this way that job analysis, job evaluation and a responsive pay system can play a constructive role in individual motivation.

Job evaluation checklist

- ■ Check that job descriptions/competency frameworks are up-to-date.
- ■ Determine the relative importance of job/person attributes.
- ■ Select an appropriate job evaluation system.
- ■ Ensure that descriptions meet the needs of the evaluation system.
- ■ Make sure that job evaluators are properly trained.
- ■ Select a representative sample of jobs for analysis.
- ■ Check data for any obvious sources of bias – for example, direct/indirect gender bias.
- ■ Ensure that evaluation factors cover key job demands.
- ■ Check that weights reflect the importance of the job.
- ■ Apply points systems, or similar, as described by the publisher.
- ■ Benchmark against other systems which reflect best practice.
- ■ Build a recognition of 'potential' into the system.
- ■ Double-check that any grade boundaries have been set fairly.
- ■ Ensure that different rates can be justified against actual job demands.

Using motivation and appraisal techniques

Perhaps the prime role of the manager is to stimulate intelligent work performance. Any techniques which provide a window on the factors which drive and motivate employees should take pride of place in the manager's 'toolkit'. Managers must discover what makes people work harder and generates corporate loyalty, and also uncover those factors which persuade people to leave. A good starting-point is to use a well constructed motivation questionnaire from a reputable test publisher. However, this information must be buttressed by face-to-face meetings and a formal process of performance appraisal.

The performance appraisal, when handled properly, is the ideal opportunity for both parties to lay their cards on the table. From a manager's perspective there is much that can be done to encourage and motivate while, at the same time, setting challenging targets. Yet, all too often, the appraisal process (if it happens at all) is a weak instrument because managers are unsure of how to carry it out and employees consider it as an imposition. The best advice that can be given in this case is that the organization should produce a proper appraisal plan linked to transparent and quantifiable objectives, and that managers should undergo professional training in how to appraise.

Job evaluation, while it has an obvious link to appraisal, is a task which requires meticulous and exhaustive research. In smaller organizations it might be reasonably straightforward to produce an equitable pay scale referenced to the local pay market, but for large organizations employing many different sorts of people the job of creating a robust pay system can be extremely complex. This, coupled with the various legal requirements, makes a good case for employing an external consultancy which specializes in reward management. They will be able to analyse the situation in a detached and objective way, and are far more likely to be seen as honest brokers than an organization's own managers.

Example MQ motivation dimensions*

Energy and dynamism

Level of activity	Invests energy readily and thrives on time pressure. Always on the go and pushing to get things done.
Achievement	Needs to achieve targets and overcome challenges. Enjoys striving to complete difficult projects.
Competition	Motivated by trying to do better than others. Comparison often spurs performance.
Fear of failure	Needs to succeed to maintain self-esteem. The possibility of failure spurs activity.
Power	Motivated when given responsibility and able to exercise authority. Demotivated by lack of opportunity to exert influence.
Immersion	Thrives on feeling involved with job. Prepared to work extended hours and invest much energy in job.
Commercial outlook	Orientation towards creating wealth and profits. Demotivated when work does not relate to results in cash terms.

Synergy

Affiliation	Thrives on meeting people, team work and helping others. Likely to feel demotivated by conflict in relationships.
Recognition	Likes to have work noticed and achievements recognised. Becomes demotivated without support.
Personal principles	Needs to feel that the organisation's work is sound. Demotivated when asked to compromise ethical standards.
Ease and security	Needs to feel secure about job and position. Does not easily tolerate unpleasant or inconvenient conditions.

* Copyright © Saville & Holdsworth Ltd (1996). This extract is from the Motivation Questionnaire expert system report. It is reproduced by permission of the publishers, Saville & Holdsworth Ltd, 3AC Court, Thames Ditton, Surrey KT7 0SR.

Personal growth	Is motivated by work which provides opportunities for development, learning and acquisition of new skills.

Intrinsic

Interest	Values stimulating and varied work. Enjoys working creatively. Demotivated by too many run of the mill tasks.
Flexibility	Favours a fluid environment without imposed structure. High tolerance of ambiguity.
Autonomy	Prefers working independently without close supervision. Demotivated when not allowed to organise own approach to work and timescales.

Extrinsic

Material reward	Links salary to success. Values perks and bonuses. Demotivated when remuneration package is poor or perceived as unfair.
Progression	Career progress, rate of promotion and just advancement are motivating.
Status	Concerned with position and status. Demotivated by lack of respect from others.

Further information

Armstrong, M. and Murlis, H. (1994), *Reward Management: A Handbook of Remuneration Strategy and Practice*, London: Kogan Page.

Fletcher, C. (1997), *Appraisal: Routes to Improved Performance*, London: Institute of Personnel and Development.

Hagemann, G. (1992), *The Motivation Manual*, Aldershot: Gower.

Ward, P. (1997), *360-Degree Feedback*, London: Institute of Personnel and Development.

Teams and Teambuilding

Overview

One of the significant trends of the last few years has been towards the creation of integrated and effective work teams which allow for the pooling of skills and abilities, the focusing of information, enhanced decision-making, and the management and control of work. When teams are carefully constructed they also have a powerful effect on the commitment and motivation of those involved. However, the dynamics of a team are highly complex and require considerable effort to understand and control. This chapter deals with the fundamental issues of the nature of teams and how they can be built. It also includes an examination of the characteristics of successful teams and the stages in their development as well as the way in which the identification of team roles can be used to stimulate performance.

The technology of teambuilding is explained through a discussion of the most influential psychological concepts and tools. Practical aspects of team development, and methods for uncovering problems with teams, are explored. The pivotal role of the leader, as the head of the organizational team, is also considered. Overall, the aim is to uncover the fundamentals of teams and teambuilding and to inform managers of the practical steps which can be taken to develop top-level teams, or the steps which can be taken to check the 'health' of existing teams.

What is a team?

Despite the popularity of the concept it is often difficult to find a satisfactory definition of a team or, rather, it is hard to formulate a descriptive phrase that applies to all types of team. Clearly all teams are concerned with a group of people working together towards some common objective, but there are many different categories of objective. Fortunately, in a business context, there are only two sorts of team which are of particular importance. These are the 'win–lose' teams, which are characteristic of sales and top-level management, and the win–win teams found in production and service delivery.

The purpose of a 'win–lose' team is to compete with other teams and to beat them. As such, the contribution of each member is directed towards the overall success of the team, usually through increasing productivity, sales or some other aspect of performance which gives the organization an edge over the opposition. Team members have an apparently symbiotic relationship as each often fills an individual, yet interdependent, role. This is especially true of top-level management teams in which senior executives have well defined areas of responsibility but are collectively responsible for the success of the organization. Teams of this nature also have a closed membership in that individuals do not simultaneously work for competitors, and are stable in the sense that individuals are always a member of the same organizational team.

In contrast 'win–win' teams are more concerned with mutual support than competition. For example, while there may be rivalry between the different shifts in a hospital, ultimately they are all concerned with achieving the same results. In fact, the hospital analogy is a good one because it highlights some of the other differences which can exist. Thus members of one team can simultaneously be members of other teams, to the extent that outside 'experts' can be called in to perform special duties, giving an open and fluid aspect to team membership. In an industrial setting the 'win–win' approach is critical to any form of production situation, as a 'win–lose' philosophy would be immensely destructive. It should also be apparent that, in healthy organizations, it is a form of teamwork that needs to operate within departments and between functions, simply because competition for resources should not be at the expense of the viability of the organization as a whole.

There are many other characteristics of teams which influence both how they work and their effectiveness. Equally, there are a number of myths about teams which hinder their development or operation. For instance, it takes considerable effort to build teams into productive units, and merely labelling a group of people as a team will not make them act like one. Similarly, teams are not usually an exercise in industrial democracy or concerned with the promotion of consensual decision-making, they are, rather, a hard-nosed attempt to concentrate talent in a specific direction and to engender group decision-making. Some additional points are listed in Table 5.1.

Virtual teams

Recently, the question of what is a team has been further complicated by the creation of so-called 'virtual teams'. In this sort of team members do not physically meet on a regular basis but interact through electronic means. Such an arrangement may sound isolating and, indeed, virtual teams do require a special form of management, but there are distinct

Table 5.1   Facts about teams

1 Ability trap
Team members should not be chosen on the grounds of intelligence alone. A preponderance of intellectuals leads to a great deal of time wasted in argument.

2 Executive fallacy
A team composed entirely of senior executives will not make better decisions! Team leaders, in particular, need to be chosen for their capability, not their seniority.

3 One location
Team members do not all have to be in the same physical location. 'Virtual' teams, using advanced IT systems, can operate across countries and even continents.

4 Team players
There is more than one type of team player. Applied research shows that there are nine main types which need to be considered – see 'Tools for team development' (pp 108–11).

5 Risky shift
Teams are better at considering problems from a number of different angles and at taking calculated risks. Individuals are frequently more cautious or careless.

6 Size matters
The maximum effective size for a team is between five and seven members. Larger teams of, say, ten or more, are harder to control and lack coherence.

7 Usefulness
Teams are good ways of pooling resources, but some problems are better tackled by individuals – for example, those problems to which there is likely to be a single solution.

8 Creative groups
When teams are composed of a number of different types of people they facilitate creative decision-making, but also produce workable ideas.

9 Team life cycle
All teams go through a series of predictable stages from start-up to disbandment. These influence the competence and cohesion of the team – see 'Building effective teams' (pp 103–8).

10 Cooperation
The single most important characteristic that all team members must share is a willingness to work together.

advantages to this form of working. First, teams can be formed regardless of whether members are in the same location. This immediately makes it possible to create complex teams which operate across and between countries. Second, the virtual nature of the team yields significant savings in terms of time and money as members do not need to travel between locations. Thus, it is easier to have access to experts and to hire people regardless of their home base. Third, in a global sense, virtual teams enable organizations to respond more quickly to whatever is happening in the business world. Finally, at a more individual level, it means that employees have greater control over the balance between their working and private lives and it makes the concept of telecommuting a viable proposition. Not only can employees work at home, or in a location remote from their office, but it allows for meaningful interactions with other co-workers or team members.

Virtual teams are rapidly being recognized as a potent way of working. However, they do depend on the right sort of technology. This centres on the use of 'groupware' or computer networks and programs which enable people to exchange data and have virtual meetings. Groupware includes:

- **E-mail and 'routing' systems**. These provide an efficient internal post system, with routing systems automatically sending information to the appropriate people.
- **Electronic folders**. Folders allow documents and data relating to a project to be grouped together. They permit all team members to view the same information and thus speed access and prevent the duplication of effort.
- **Automatic audit trails**. Audit systems track the current status of a project and monitor performance. This means that issues of quality and process performance can be dealt with while the project is underway.
- **Conferencing**. Videoconferencing allows team members working in remote locations to discuss a project with their colleagues in a 'virtual' conference room. Likewise, teleconferencing systems can connect users, using an audio link.

All these developments mean that it is now possible to connect all the people in a team – or for that matter in an organization – through a network into one electronic work group. However, while technology is important it does not, by itself, make virtual teams work. They require, if anything, a greater exchange of information than traditional teams, and certainly greater clarity of purpose. This is partly because of the lack of physical interaction and the loss of much non-verbal communication, but also because they are a characterized by a different sort of team cohesion. As a result, although virtual teams allow greater flexibility and free organizations from the constraints of fixed working hours and the availability of people in particular offices, they require a formal method of development and management. Care must be taken to create good and trusting relationships between team members before they begin to operate in a virtual world. This is best done through traditional teambuilding exercises, as described later in this chapter (see pp 109–11), and by making the virtual team leader a facilitator and 'knowledge' manager. This means that the leader must actively manage each member's personal development (which is crucial for maintaining high levels of motivation and energy) and also implement strategy through a debate with team members using the information that is common to all of them. In short, the role of the leader, and of the virtual team itself, is to integrate people, work processes, strategy and technology.

The development of virtual teams and the associated technology is a specialist area. Any organization considering this form of team working is well advised to contact a specialist consultancy. A useful starting-point is the *Knowledge Associates* website (www.knowledgeassociates.com).

Building effective teams

Teambuilding needs to be centred on specific and identifiable tasks, preferably genuine work problems or exercises which can simulate important aspects of the team process. The task of building a team is also enhanced by using a group of people who will actually have to work together in the future, rather than an artificial grouping of individuals. Furthermore, research has shown that effective teams are not static but adapt to the task at hand. For example, a large project will move through a number of different phases, with each phase requiring a team with a slightly different composition and brief. As a result, teambuilding needs to cover a least five main areas:

■ **Task management.** The approach adopted by the team needs to be systematic and to include formal objective-setting, planning and organizing, time management, problem-solving and review. In some cases – for example, with time management or aspects of problem-solving – team members may need additional training. It should also be recognized that many of these activities need to take place on a cyclical basis, in particular, the act of reviewing progress is likely to influence the management of subsequent phases of a project.
■ **Process management.** In a psychological sense this involves interpersonal competencies such as questioning, listening, summarizing, encouraging, conflict resolution and so on. As before, these may need to be 'taught' or, at the very least, team members will need to practice operating in a collaborative way. For example, it is unwise to assume that team members will automatically listen to each other. This is an

important issue as a problem in this area often leads to duplication of effort and the inefficient use of resources.

■ **Intergroup communication**. As teams seldom exist in isolation it is necessary to develop a mechanism for communication with other teams, functions or work groups. This requires negotiating skills, political know-how and an understanding of the 'win–lose', 'win–win' distinction made earlier.

■ **Team style**. All teams are different because of the people that make them up, and the ways in which they interact with each other and the outside world. The team's task will also affect how people behave and the roles they choose to take. This makes it important that team leaders and coordinators adopt an appropriate managerial style – one which matches both the needs of the team and those of the situation.

■ **Contribution management**. The skills, abilities, personality and expertise of each team member must be understood since these form the basis of an individual's 'team role' and helps identify their unique qualities. Team leaders, in particular, need to appreciate what each person has to offer, and to manage the team so that all members have an opportunity to contribute.

Stages of team development

From a purely functional point of view, managers should understand that, during team development, members go through a number of clearly identifiable stages. Indeed, many training programmes are based on a five-stage model concerned with 'forming', 'storming', 'norming', 'performing' and 'mourning' (see Figure 5.1).

In the 'forming' stage team members behave as a group of enthusiastic individuals. Their commitment is often high, but the lack of any significant 'gelling' usually means that little gets done. Often a great deal of time is spent on discussing ways of operating and on establishing relationships. At this stage, the team can be considered to be undeveloped and, as members are unsure of each other, exchanges are frequently too polite and deferential.

Once the team has become established it moves into a 'storming' stage which is often characterized by disagreements, interpersonal conflict and a questioning of individual roles and responsibilities. This can be considered to be a period of experimentation and is important if the team is to move on. The golden rule at this stage is not to assume that conflict is counterproductive but, rather, an essential process through which the team learns about itself. Indeed, be wary of any team in which the members claim that there has never been any conflict.

When the team moves out of the 'storming' stage a consensus emerges. This is termed 'norming' because team members are now focused and

Figure 5.1   Stages of team development

agreed on a way of proceeding. The real work starts to be carried out, and trust develops between team members. It is now possible to observe increased commitment (in contrast to the 'storming' stage in which it frequently drops) as well as competent decision-making and better performance.

Finally the team moves into a mature 'performing' stage in which competency has been firmly established. The team operates in an open and flexible way and deals with disagreements and conflict in a constructive manner. There may also be an emphasis on the development of individual members. However, if the identity of the team is broken through the loss of members, or its imminent disbanding, commitment and performance can drop quickly. In such circumstances the team may move into a fifth stage, that of 'mourning'. Yet, paradoxically, sometimes the demise of a team, if it is coupled with the rise of another, can lead to an *increase* in commitment and activity. The energy generated by a second process of 'forming' can then lead to quicker progress towards effective working.

The identification of these stages is of considerable practical interest. They provide a basis for understanding why teams behave in the way that they do and allow managers to pre-empt some of the obvious frictions inherent in team development. When placed alongside the topics that need to be considered in teambuilding programmes, they suggest three key principles for development:

1 **Prepare team members.** It is unrealistic to expect people to move seamlessly from working as individuals to being members of a team. They need time to get used to the idea and to understand what is involved. Some of the skills required for teamworking may need to be taught, and this will take more time. Furthermore, some people may resent the idea of being placed in a team and take it as an indication of a lack of personal competence. If this is the case, this perception needs to be dealt with quickly and firmly before the team actually forms. All these considerations point towards a structured process of teambuilding and an organization will therefore require trained facilitators or need to retain the services of a consultancy with experience of teambuilding.

2 **Clarify the team's objectives.** A great deal of the time which is wasted, and the friction which emerges, during the 'forming' and 'storming' stages, can be short-circuited by establishing a start-up strategy. This involves giving the team a method for approaching the problem with which it is tasked, or a 'process consultant'. The former is often achieved by running a team development workshop over a number of days; the latter by co-opting a consultant who acts as a 'ring master' and keeps the team on target.

3 **Set measurable targets.** Many teams flounder because they are not sure what they are supposed to be achieving. It is extremely important to set clear objectives, have an explicit method for the team to measure its own progress and identify aims and objectives before matters of process are considered, otherwise teams often agree on the way in which they would like to achieve a set of (notional) objectives, without clearly identifying what they are supposed to be!

Team roles

Much team development activity is based on the work of the UK management scientist, Meredith Belbin who conducted studies at the Administrative Staff College in Henley and identified a number of team types, or roles, which are characteristic of successful teams. The nine roles he described now form the basis of many questionnaires used in teambuilding. Table 5.2 provides brief descriptions of the nine team roles.

Belbin's work on management teams also highlights the fact that different types of project require different sorts of team, and that, in effective teams, members should fulfil a number of roles. Whilst it is not necessary for all nine roles to be represented in every team, teams do require a

Table 5.2   Belbin's team roles

	Personal attributes	Contribution to team
Leaders		
1 Coordinator	Calm, mature, confident controlled, social leader	Clarifies objectives, sets agenda, encourages contributions
2 Shaper	Outgoing, challenging, dynamic, highly strung	Challenges inertia, pushes boundaries, energizes
Thinkers		
3 Monitor–Evaluator	Sober, strategic, discreet, unemotional	Analyses problems, interprets data, assesses contributions
4 Plant	Imaginative, individualistic, unorthodox, intellectual	Makes proposals, criticizes, offers new insights
Brokers		
5 Team worker	Social, perceptive, mild, accommodating	Responds to others, strong sense of purpose, team 'cement'
6 Resource Investigator	Curious, communicative, extroverted, enthusiastic	Negotiates outside team, sells ideas, acts as 'diplomat'
Organizers		
7 Co-implementer	Reliable, conservative, disciplined, efficient	Applies common sense, turns ideas into action, prioritizes
8 Completer	Careful, orderly, anxious, conscientious	Supports others, builds on ideas, perfectionist
Specialists	Dedicated, self-starter, focused	Brings knowledge and expertise, adds specialist capability

These descriptions are based on Belbin's nine team roles. For further information see his book, *Team Roles at Work*, published by Butterworth Heinemann (1993).

good spread of personnel. In Table 5.2 I have grouped team roles into five main areas – 'leaders', 'thinkers', 'brokers' and 'organizers' – which is the minimum spread required by an effective team. In technical situations a 'specialist' will also be required. Belbin also observed that a 'full set' of team roles is most critical in situations of rapid change, whereas, in stable circumstances, teams can often function effectively with some elements missing.

Although this method of classifying team roles is very seductive, it should not be applied rigidly as this can lead to unhelpful stereotyping and the overlooking of potential. In reality, people often do not fit neatly into just one of Belbin's roles – an individual may, for example, have both excellent thinking and broking skills. Furthermore, in a small team, members will have to play a number of different roles and, in a very large team, many roles will be duplicated. In the latter case it is advisable to split the team into smaller working groups, with the whole team meeting just to review progress. All this implies that teambuilding is not just a question of acknowledging roles at a superficial level, but of moulding teams according to size, purpose and the pool of potential talent.

With an already existing team the Belbin approach can help discover its strengths and limitations – an important exercise since many organizations do not have the luxury of picking teams on the basis of personal qualities, but assemble them on the basis of function. The process of exploring the way in which a team operates can also help explain the reasons for underperformance: there may be no-one filling an important team role or there may be too many competing for a single role. For example, if the majority of members are trying to fill 'thinker' roles, the team's output will often be disappointing. This is because individualists, or those with a strongly competitive streak, do not work well in teams unless they are matched with those who are more practical or organizationally skilled. This is one reason why 'think tanks', or supposedly expert groups, often fail to live up to expectations.

Tools for team development

There are several ways of discovering how someone will behave in a team. It is possible, for example, to review how they have worked in teams in the past. This can be achieved through a process of performance appraisal or by directly asking managers and team leaders. However, this will only provide a form of historical information, and there may be a number of purely subjective reasons why someone is perceived as being a 'good' or 'poor' team member. For instance, team leaders often rate performance highly if individuals mirror the way in which they themselves operate and, conversely, mark down those who are more abrasive or independently minded. Unfortunately this usually happens at the expense of the person's actual contribution to the team. This means that it is often best to use some form of structured assessment.

Most of the popular personality questionnaires such as the *16PF™* and *OPQ®* can be used to generate information on team roles and, for illustration purposes, an extract from an *OPQ®* report is provided at the end of the chapter. Other questionnaires have been designed specifically to assess team role behaviour. Belbin's original *Team Role Self-Perception Inventory* is reproduced at the end of his best-selling book, *Management Teams: Why They Succeed or Fail* and, more recently, he has produced a multi-rater inventory called *Interface IV* which is available from Belbin Associates which is based in Cambridge, UK. Other titles to look out for are the *Types of Work Index* (TWI) and *Team Management Index* (TMI) designed by Charles Margerison and Dick McCann of the UK-based consultancy, Team Management Systems. Their TMI is based on eight types: explorer–promoter; assessor–developer; thruster–organizer; concluder–producer; checker–inspector; upholder–maintainer; reporter–advisor; and creator–innovator. The origins of this system are in Jungian psychology which is also the theory used to produce one of the most influential measures of individual personality, the *Myers-Briggs Type Indicator™* (MBTI™). The MBTI is discussed in some detail in Chapter 6. Finally, a questionnaire called *FIRO–B™* (Fundamental Interpersonal Relationship Orientation–Behaviour), which assesses social behaviour and needs, is also widely used in team development. This is distributed by the US publisher, Consulting Psychologists Press Inc., and is available in the UK from Oxford Psychologists Press.

Although there seems to be a plethora of different questionnaires for deciding how someone will behave in a team situation, they all work by categorizing individuals, and each of those mentioned can be used for personal development or for creating 'balanced' work or management teams. The one that you use depends entirely on which theory you select but, whatever your choice, it is important to realize that questionnaires are only indicators: they demonstrate preference and are not absolute measures of team role. Consequently, it would be unwise indeed to slavishly apply team questionnaire results.

Team development exercises

A selection of team-oriented questionnaires are often combined with other activities to form a development programme. These typically last two or three days and are designed to weld a group of individuals into a functioning team. Often this involves the use of outdoor exercises in which team members are placed under a certain degree of pressure and have to rely on each other in order to complete a series of tasks. The classic example is transporting all the members of a team over a river using a selection of ropes, planks and oil drums. Similar exercises, involving construction tasks, can also take place indoors. For example, the team may be supplied with a range of everyday materials and be asked to design a mechanism for 'rescuing' an egg. In this scenario an egg is suspended from the ceiling and the team has to devise a way of catching it, without damage, when the string is cut after a given period of time. Such practical exercises, when used in combination with more analytical business-based tasks, give participants an opportunity to see how teams operate. They also provide a safe environment in which to experiment with new ways of working. Furthermore, completing 'non-work' tasks can often be extremely revealing as, of course, can the act of living with other team members for a number of days.

Team development exercises work best if there are sufficient participants for at least two teams. An example timetable for the first day of a teambuilding programme is presented below. Such a programme would require two or three trained facilitators.

Team Development Programme

Day 1

09:00 Introduction: objectives of the development programme
09:30 Personal introductions: participants introduce themselves
10:00 Short presentation: teams and the process of teamwork
10:30 Building a bridge: teams compete against each other and the clock
12:00 Bridge process review 1: feedback from facilitators
12:30 Lunch
13:30 Bridge process review 2: teams discuss performance
14:00 Bridge video review: teams watch video of exercise
14:45 Team feedback: team members give each other feedback
15:30 Tea
16:00 Analytical exercise: based on business scenario.
17:00 Analytical process review 1: feedback from facilitators
17:30 Analytical process review 2: teams discuss performance
18:00 Egg rescue: teams devise a way to save an egg
19:00 Dinner
20:00 Egg process review 1: feedback from facilitators
20:30 Egg process review 2: teams discuss performance
21:00 Questionnaires: participants complete personality questionnaires
22:00 Day ends

The second day would include additional input on team processes and feedback on the questionnaires completed by the participants. There would also be a discussion and an exercise concerned with creating 'balanced' teams, using Belbin's team roles or a similar classification system. Team development exercises should be designed to push participants and move them out of their 'comfort zone.' In addition, a degree of tension can be introduced by getting teams to work long (but not excessive) hours. This has the effect of highlighting how teams work when the members are tired and slightly stressed. However, whatever the structure of the programme, it is extremely important that it is fun. In light of this, exercises should be physically safe and relatively non-confrontational; the inclusion of social activities can also make the whole experience more enjoyable.

Team development checklist

- Brief participants on developmental aims and objectives.
- Ensure that participants know what physical activities to expect.
- Produce a detailed programme for participants and facilitators.
- Check that you have enough suitably trained facilitators.
- Make sure that the venue is properly equipped and supervised.
- Use a combination of practical and analytical exercises.
- Conduct process reviews after each exercise.
- Use questionnaires to gather information on team behaviour.
- Always relate exercise feedback to participants' work context.
- Include a thorough debrief on the last day.
- Follow up participants after the training event.
- Make the training event fun but do not give the impression that it is just a social event.

Top teams

At a fundamental level, top teams are composed of members who trust and respect each other. This may sound self-evident, but the issue of trust is central to good team functioning and is of particular importance for multinational teams who may rarely meet face-to-face, although some of the IT developments mentioned earlier can help to alleviate this problem. It is also a factor that differentiates between high and low performance sports and military teams. This is most apparent if you consider the functioning of an aerobatics display team, which relies on immense skill and complete trust.

Top-level teams have an extremely clear view of their purpose. The members know why the team was formed, what it is intended to do, the resources which are available to complete the task at hand, how performance will be measured and what will constitute success. In many teams this clarity of purpose is reinforced by an effective leader or, in Belbin's terms, a skilled 'coordinator'. This is a charismatic individual who has the ability to generate team spirit and an understanding of how to tap into each member's unique abilities. Excellent teams also contain a foil to the coordinator in the form of an ideas person, or somebody who can give a new insight into problems (a 'plant').

A winning team is also characterized by team members who are fulfilling their preferred roles and therefore playing to their strengths, rather than being forced to play certain roles simply because they have done so in the past. All this is related to an understanding of the team process in which the members sense problems within the team and resolve them by compensating for any weaknesses – a mechanism which obviously works better if there is a good spread of abilities and roles within the team. The same mechanism can also protect against team members competing with each other, and help allocate individuals to non-conflicting activities. In short, the team has a way of monitoring itself and of maintaining a state of dynamic equilibrium.

Finally, top teams guard against the dangers of 'group think'. This is a condition in which the team culture becomes so strong that it tends to overpower the team's purpose. The symptoms include:

- **Rationalization**. Inconvenient facts or information which does not fit with the team's view are explained away.
- **Conformity**. The power to conform is so strong that no individual member is prepared to challenge decisions.
- **Collectivity**. This is related to conformity and is concerned with a fixation on collective responsibility.
- **Censorship**. The team censors its own process and presents a sanitized picture of itself to the outside world.
- **Invulnerability**. The team begins to believe its own propaganda and assumes that it is the only group which can solve a particular problem.
- **Stereotyping**. Highly conforming teams often stereotype, frequently inaccurately, those with whom they consider themselves to be in competition.

The problems of 'group think' often afflict high-level teams such as boards of directors. In fact, the above list was partly derived from a US analysis of the 'Bay of Pigs' fiasco – one of the many unsuccessful plots to assassinate the Cuban leader, Fidel Castro – planned by the most influential and skilled strategists in the Kennedy administration. The moral is that such groups, whether they be governmental or business-oriented, must actively encourage self-criticism, look outside for information and deal objectively with conflicting data. From a corporate point of view, this suggests that top-level teams should have non-executive members – individuals who can bring an external perspective to the functioning of the team.

Case study: the spaghetti bridge

An advanced teambuilding course was run for the senior executives of an international engineering group. On the first day the ten participants were split into two groups. The first group was composed of those with a professional engineering background, the second of a range of individuals, none of whom had specialist engineering training. The task was to build the most 'cost effective' free-standing bridge across a one metre gap, using a range of materials supplied by the facilitators. The materials, which attracted varying costs, included:

- drinking straws
- plastic cups
- cotton thread
- pins
- paper clips
- rubber bands
- sheets of A5 card
- sticky tape
- uncooked spaghetti.

The two teams were given 40 minutes to produce a costed design for the bridge. When this was approved the teams had a further 40 minutes to build the structure. Any changes to the design during the construction phase, or requests for further materials, attracted penalties. The structure was then tested to destruction by loading the middle with coins. Before the teams began the task the facilitators made themselves available to discuss the relative merits of different sorts of bridges – namely, 'arch', 'cantilever' and 'suspension' designs. The engineering group declined any advice. The facilitators also suggested that, given the scale of the bridge, uncooked spaghetti would exhibit the same physical properties as high tensile steel.

After 80 minutes two bridges had been built. The engineering group had constructed a suspension bridge using spaghetti, the non-specialist group a simple design based on strength rather than elegance. The spaghetti bridge collapsed.

The main point of this case is that the top-level team, which immediately adopted the most complicated design, indulged in many aspects of 'group think'. They were closed to outside influences (invulnerability), accepted what had been said about spaghetti despite some initial doubts (rationalized), made fun of the other group (stereotyped), and all believed until the end that they had produced the better bridge.

Epilogue: One member of the engineering group was so distressed that the bridge had failed that he built another (working) version and presented it to the facilitators on the last day of the course.

Team leaders

Some commentators consider the topic of leadership to be quite distinct from that of teams and teambuilding. However, teams require a focus and it seems sensible to assume that leaders, of whatever type, require a cohesive group of people to lead. As a result, indicators of leadership style are frequently found in team role questionnaires or more general assessments of managerial approach.

In Chapter 1, p. 23 the concepts of 'transactional' and 'transformational' leadership were introduced and, in a similar way, Belbin's categorization distinguishes between the 'shaper' and the 'coordinator'. However, these distinctions simplify a complicated topic and there are at least five main forms of leadership behaviour. One widely used classification divides leaders into the following categories:

- **Directive**. This type of leader has a clear personal vision of what is required and keeps tight control over the activities of the team. He or she maintains sole responsibility for strategy development, planning and control. This style is preferred by team members who do not wish to be concerned with internal team management.
- **Delegative**. The delegative leader adopts a 'hands-off' approach and allows team members to take responsibility for projects. However, he or she is not necessarily democratic, and projects may be assigned without sufficient thought. On balance, this approach is preferred by team members who are naturally independent, but casts those who require direct supervision adrift.
- **Participative**. As the name implies, a participative approach is characterized by involvement and a democratic team structure. This type of leader favours consensual decision-making and is prepared to take time over important decisions. This style can be anathema to team members who hold strong personal views, or those who want immediate action.
- **Consultative**. The consultative leader is concerned with the views of the team and makes space for members to be heard. However, unlike the participative leader, he or she retains a firm grip on planning and control and makes the final decisions. The 'steer' which this gives to group activities can be an irritant to more self-reliant team members.
- **Negotiative**. This type of leader relies heavily on negotiation skills and deal-making to achieve team objectives. Thus members will be encouraged to act through the use of incentives or an appeal to their particular needs or wants. This is another flexible approach; it resembles the participative style, but relies on the direct manipulation of the team. At times, it leads to unconventional ways of motivating team members.

When considering leadership, or selecting a leader, consideration should also be given to adaptability, or the degree to which a leader can switch between different sorts of behaviour depending on the circumstances. For example, sometimes a leader needs to be directive and play an active role in channelling the team's energies whereas, at other times, a more consultative and transformational style may be more appropriate. The trick is to identify a leader who has this capability and not one who can only operate in a single mode. Business history, and of course politics, is littered with countless examples of the latter. The following description of leadership style, based on a well known personality questionnaire, may well sound familiar.

Example: leadership narrative

Primary style
X is an extremely directive leader. She has a particularly clear view of the objectives of the team and makes it obvious what is required of its members. A great deal of effort will be put into developing a plan for the team but, paradoxically, she is unlikely to keep a close watch on how members perform their tasks. This is coupled with a disregard for the opinions of other team members and an unshakable belief in the correctness of her own views. This lack of interest is contrasted with a deep interest in what makes people 'tick' and a concern for how her own management style is viewed. At times, team members will be expected to reinforce her view that the only way to achieve results is to support her as a leader.

Secondary style
X can play the role of the negotiative leader when required. She has well developed bargaining skills and can identify competitors' weak points. From a team perspective she is adept at energizing members by recognizing the best way of achieving the reaction she seeks. As a result, she can disguise her natural tendency to issue instructions, or to command others, as long as the team is moving in the direction which she desires. At other times, she will achieve results by doing deals with individual team members and drive the team forward by cultivating a spirit of competition. Overall, her style is ambitious and competitive, and a great deal of energy will be put into making the team a success.

Adaptability
Despite the fact that X can adopt two different leadership roles, these are both directive in nature. This means that, in circumstances where real compromise is required, she will find it difficult to accept an alternative point of view. While this can be a strength in some negotiation situations it will ultimately lead to inflexible and isolated decision-making. X should

aim to develop a more participative or consultative style, or to delegate some decision-making to a more adaptable deputy.

Team health check

It is good management practice to occasionally check on the functioning of existing teams. This can be achieved by conducting a diagnostic survey focused on each team member's view of the team's objectives, team process and interpersonal 'chemistry' (or how the team members interact with each other). A comprehensive survey will also ask the team's 'customers' or 'clients' for their views on the same issues.

In practical terms the survey should comprise a series of statements which relate to effective team functioning. To generate useful results it is also advisable to give respondents the opportunity to rate statements using a suitable scale – say, a five-point rating scale ranging from 'totally untrue', through 'sometimes true', to 'always true'. Allowing respondents to answer in this way will produce more meaningful results and will highlight those areas of team functioning which require attention.

Some example statements are listed below, but note that surveys should be relatively short and only contain about 15 or 20 items.

Objectives – 1

■ Group objectives are clear and written down.
■ We all understand the objectives of the group.
■ We review objectives on a regular basis.
■ We always achieve group objectives on time.

Process – 1

■ We all have clearly assigned roles.
■ New tasks are allocated without argument.
■ The team coordinates its own activities.
■ Problems in the team are identified early.

Process – 2

■ We have a method of monitoring progress.
■ We know when we have met our objectives.
■ We actively respond to 'customer' complaints.
■ The timing for individual tasks is known.

Process – 3

■ The team welcomes new information and ideas.
■ The team has efficient problem-solving methods.

- Everyone is involved in decision-making.
- Team decisions are taken promptly.

Interpersonal

- Team members support each other.
- Team members enjoy working together.
- Team members accept constructive criticism.
- Everyone feels that their contribution is recognized.

This is by no means an exhaustive list and further statements could be generated for personal involvement, learning and development. It should also be recognized that team loyalties will affect the way in which surveys are completed so that even when things are going wrong ratings can still seem to be positive. Because of this, when results are totalled, it is wise to concentrate on the relative differences between results rather than the size of the scores. This will help underline the differences between different aspects of, say, team process, rather than give a false impression based on the fact that ratings are all towards the top end of the scale.

Using teambuilding techniques

There are many excellent resources available for teambuilding. These range from questionnaires and other psychometric measures to complex simulation exercises which take place over a number of days. All can be used by appropriately trained personnel or accessed through test publishers and consultancy firms. However, teambuilding is not a magic solution to such problems as low productivity or poor communication; it only works if there is a genuine commitment to change. It is very easy to design a team development programme which is enjoyable, well received and which makes no difference to workplace behaviour at all!

The question to ask is why the organization is interested in teamworking, and moreover whether the will exists to let people work in teams at all. The latter is an important point because many organizations claim to promote a team approach and yet retain most of their old work style so that the balance of individual tasks far outweighs those which take place within the team. Equally, it is still uncommon for pay to be based on the activity of the team as a whole; it is far more likely to be linked to individual performance.

As with many of the other techniques described in this book it is simple to apply teambuilding approaches in a crude and ill-directed fashion. To be effective they need to be seen as part of the development solution, not the solution itself. Team development is a long-term process related to selection and assessment, motivation and performance appraisal, individual and organizational learning – all need to be addressed in order to create the right climate for teams to flourish.

Example OPQ® team role narrative*

Occupational Personality Questionnaire Expert System

Automated Narrative Report

Concept 4.2

Mr Robert Fraser

- 11- Jun-97 -

Team Type Styles

Style	Description
Co-ordinator	■ Sets the team goals and defines roles. ■ Co-ordinates team efforts and leads by eliciting respect.
Shaper	■ The task leader who brings competitive drive to the team. ■ Makes things happen but may be thought abrasive
Plant	■ Imaginative, intelligent and the team's source of original ideas. ■ Concerned with fundamentals
Monitor Evaluator	■ Offers measured, dispassionate critical analysis. ■ Keeps team from pursuing misguided objectives.
Resource Investigator	■ Sales person, diplomat, resource seeker. ■ Good improviser with many external contacts. ■ May be easily diverted from task in hand.
Completer	■ Worries about problems. Personally checks details. ■ Intolerant of the casual and the slapdash. Sees projects through.
Team Worker	■ Promotes team harmony. Good listener who builds on ideas. ■ Likeable and assertive.
Implementer	■ Turns decisions and strategies into manageable tasks. ■ Brings logical, methodical pursuit of objectives to the team.

Team Behaviour

The text below describes Mr Fraser's likely behaviour when working as part of a team, by linking his preferred style to various Team Types. It may prove useful to refer to Mr Fraser's full OPQ profile when interpreting the following report.*

Mr Fraser very much enjoys taking the role of co-ordinator in a team. As such he is likely to be enthusiastic and goal-orientated. Interestingly, Mr Fraser is also quite happy to behave as the shaper in a group. He has great need for achievement and is likely to set challenging targets. His concern is to win and he will put every effort into the process.

Whereas shapers are primarily focused on the meeting of objectives, the co-ordinator in Mr Fraser will mean that he will seek to do this by appealing to the motives of other members of the team. Similarly, the positive approach of the co-ordinator may soften in him what can be impatience and a tendency, typical of shapers, to argue strongly for his own views. Hopefully, therefore, this combination of co-ordinator and shaper roles will allow Mr Fraser to combine effectively his orientation towards the achievement of goals with some focus on the stable maintenance of the team.

However, it is possible that Mr Fraser's desire to achieve the team's objectives may be at the expense of the feelings of other team members, who may find him abrasive. He may show his frustration if he feels that others are obstructing his pursuit of his goals. The shaper can be invaluable when the team lacks direction, but he can inhibit the performance of a smoothly-functioning team. Not only is Mr Fraser happy to play the role of both co-ordinator and shaper, but he may also emerge as the team's plant, generating ideas. He sees himself as quite creative and innovative. Mr Fraser may not always be a team player in the first instance, however, and his ideas may have to be drawn out of him.

Mr Fraser may usefully combine some of his co-ordinating behaviours with his inclination to come up with ideas, for example, by actively asking others what they think of his suggestions, or by relying on other people's views to spark off additional ideas. However, the fact that Mr Fraser is a shaper may emphasise his degree of goal-orientation and his need to take charge, as well as the degree to which he thinks independently of others. This tendency is therefore likely to add a harder edge to his creative and co-ordinating approach. Interestingly, Mr Fraser possesses many traits which complement his behaviour as a possible plant, and suggest that he would be adept in the role of resource investigator. Therefore, he may not only come up with novel ideas, but may actively make them work by gathering information which allows decisions about feasibility and strategy to be made. By contrast with the typical plant, he may also be quite extrovert and confident, having no reservations about exploring beyond the team itself and probing others for information.

The picture of Mr Fraser is therefore of someone who is innovative in a broad sense, who combines an orientation towards in-depth and creative thinking with an ability to focus on the external liaison necessary to make his ideas work. His contacts and sources outside the team may also make him a good improviser, capable of enlisting outside help if things don't go according to plan. Mr Fraser is inquisitive, but his enthusiasm for a particular issue may be short-lived, particularly if he does not receive stimulation from others.

Mr Fraser's role as a co-ordinator is enhanced by his willingness to liaise outside the team, thereby combining a broad understanding of the team's strengths with an appreciation of those external resources which may complement them.

* See 'Example OPQ narrative report', pp 73–6.

He should be aware that his combination of plant and shaper characteristics may result in him upsetting others by passionately proposing his own ideas, perhaps in preference to others' suggestions. While Mr Fraser gets some satisfaction from the opportunity to generate ideas and liaise with external contacts, he does see himself as a monitor evaluator and therefore derives less enjoyment from the process of objective decision-making. While he may be able in this regard, he is unlikely to see his strength as sitting back and offering dispassionate feedback on how well the team is pursuing its objectives. This means that another member of the team may need to offer such contributions and promote consideration of the pros and cons of various options. Furthermore, he may sometimes be more emotionally involved and committed to the outcome of decisions than is typical of a monitor evaluator.

Given his relative lack of enthusiasm for objective analysis, it is perhaps surprising that Mr Fraser demonstrates very little concern for the 'people' aspects of group work. This is despite a fairly sociable and diplomatic orientation towards others. Therefore, Mr Fraser is unlikely to be the one who calms people down and averts further problems, in the way that a typical team worker might do.

While Mr Fraser is likely to be the originator of a wide range of ideas, his lack of impartial consideration of these before communicating them to the team may mean that many of these suggestions are too radical or impractical to gain acceptance. Because many of his proposals are turned down he may need careful handling by other members of the team to ensure that his motivation is maintained, and that his more practical ideas are capitalised upon. Mr Fraser is likely to be much more concerned with encouraging good communication within the team and gathering team members' opinions than in probing or evaluating. He needs to be supportive of the more critical and objective members of the team and ensure that they are allowed to have their say, whilst giving recognition to the skills of all team members. Somewhat in keeping with his relative disinterest in a highly objective and analytic approach to decision making is some unwillingness on Mr Fraser's part to act as the implementer in a team. He may not be particularly conscientious, and he is perhaps anxious to move on to the next thing. While he may therefore come up with novel ideas himself, another team member is likely to have to implement them.

In a similar vein, Mr Fraser is not likely to adopt the role of completer. He is unlikely to enjoy having to tie up loose ends and is likely to have less concern than others to ensure that the back-up activities associated with a project are planned into schedules. He may furthermore see himself as being somewhat flexible about deadlines, occasionally letting matters go unfinished. As is often the case, while Mr Fraser is very interested in maintaining a wide circle of external contacts, he has less interest in seeing the project through. Indeed, it may well be that he is so preoccupied with keeping in touch that deadlines may be overlooked. Mr Fraser will probably spend time involving all members of the team in decision making and goal-setting, but having done this is unlikely to focus upon organising the more detailed aspects of the project which consequently may not be completed to schedule.

Further information

Belbin, R. M. (1981), *Management Teams: Why They Succeed or Fail*, London: Heinemann.

Owen, H. (1996), *Creating Top Flight Teams*, London: Kogan Page.

Parker, G. and Kropp, R. (1985), *Team Building: A Sourcebook of Activities for Trainers*, London: Kogan Page.
Woodcock, M. (1989), *Team Development Manual*, Aldershot: Gower.

Training and Management Development

Overview

The founder of IBM, Thomas Watson, believed that an organization's investment in education and training was directly related to its rate of growth. He was often quoted as saying that between 40 and 50 per cent of management time should be devoted to educating and motivating employees. Many managers find this a startling figure, but business growth depends on employee development keeping pace with changes in the marketplace.

This chapter looks at the role of training and ways of identifying training needs. Consideration is given to different forms of development, such as on-the-job training, and techniques for evaluating their effectiveness, the latter being of considerable importance as many companies invest substantial resources in training programmes and yet have no mechanism for determining their effectiveness. Next, the issue of management development is explored, with particular attention being given to the use of the 'development centre'.

Finally, the focus moves to matters of personal development and career management – in particular, the ways in which continuing professional development and mentoring not only benefit the individual but enhance the effectiveness of the entire organization.

The role of training

The role of training is to enable an organization to achieve its strategic goals through increasing productivity and efficiency, and by broadening its pool of talent and capability. This often involves adopting new ways of working, or producing changes in attitudes and behaviour which allow meaningful change to take place. In addition, more enlightened organizations understand that the financial return from training is better considered in 'pay-forward' rather than 'pay-back' terms. A pay-back approach, based on the accountancy notion of 'direct return', involves a straightforward financial calculation of the impact of training. This can, of course, be expressed through changes to turnover, profit, sales or some other similar indicator. As long as an organization has a reliable way of measuring such things, evidence can then be provided on the time period over which an investment in training produces results. However, while pay-back calculations may appear to be an obvious method of evaluation there are often problems in assessing performance prior to a training intervention, and assessing the true cost of the training itself. This is because training involves transparent costs such as those attached to tutors and facilities, and less quantifiable costs like those involved in lost 'production' (while the training is taking place) and follow-up coaching and monitoring.

In contrast, the pay-forward view of training emphasizes the return in terms of cultural change, increases in employee loyalty, clearer identification with business objectives and observable changes in individual and group behaviour. These are all factors which are difficult to express in monetary terms, but genuinely improve an organization's ability to learn and change.

Thus investments in training are not designed to be an end in themselves, but a way of moving an organization forward in a much broader and integrated way. Students of organizational change will no doubt see the parallel between training described in these terms and the work of Peter Senge on the 'learning organization'. In his 1990 book, *The Fifth Discipline* (New York: Doubleday), he highlights the difference between training as an episodic event designed for distinct groups of people, and the learning organization which promotes individual learning as a continuous process. As already noted, it is more difficult to demonstrate the financial return that comes from such a pay-forward approach, but it is possible to monitor through the use of surveys and feedback questionnaires. It is also feasible to mix what appear to be pay-forward and pay-back approaches. For example, some companies – particularly in the manufacturing sector – invest heavily in on-the-job training and also support individual learning. In these organizations it is not unusual for 50 per cent of employees to be engaged in individual learning at any one time. Furthermore, while most of this learning is generally related to the companies' activities, it does not have to be specifically job-focused. The promotion of self-development in this way is the mark of an organization with a high degree of training maturity – one that realizes that employees who are motivated to learn, and develop, are, in turn, more productive.

Obviously not all businesses are ready to embrace the notion of the learning organization, but it is still useful to assess a company's current level of training 'maturity'. One way of doing this is to determine the sort of training typically offered within an organization. This can range from no systematic training at all, to training which is used as an arm of organizational strategy. The distinctions used by consultants are presented in Table 6.1.

Table 6.1   Training maturity

Zero training	Some organizations have no systematic training programme. In this situation it is important to know if this is a deliberate policy (and why), or whether it is merely the result of inertia. Analysis should focus on any opportunities lost through lack of training and the potential pay-back from introducing some form of training.
Tactical training	This is training which is linked to specific job competencies. Consequently, it is necessary to establish that well defined performance indicators and measures are in place. Analysis should focus on whether the right sort of training is being given (are different types prioritized?), and whether pay-back information is available.
Operational training	In this case training is keyed to an operational plan linked to individual career development. Training objectives are supported by senior managers and outcomes formally assessed. Analysis should focus on whether training objectives reflect manpower policy, and if appraisal systems take into account performance, learning needs and pay-forward gains.
Corporate training	Training has a corporate function and is seen as a means of implementing change. It is accepted as a way of underpinning things like quality and cultural change programmes. Analysis should focus on the adequacy of pay-forward assessments, and whether training is developing at the same speed as the business.
Strategic training	This form of training directly couples development activities with the formation of strategy. The learning process is used to inform strategic aims and objectives.

Cont.

Analysis should concentrate on the degree to which learning is viewed as a corporate asset, and the extent to which it produces a continuous (pay-forward) return.

Learning organization   In the learning organization training is used to formulate strategy. Learning is seen to produce a competitive advantage in its own right.

Analyses should focus on the distinction between training and management (which should disappear), and whether an organization ceases to think in pay-back terms.

This table is based on work by John Burgoyne. A more detailed analysis can be found in his article, 'Management Development for the Individual and the Organization', published in *Personnel Management*, June 1988.

Training needs analysis (TNA)

Training needs analysis (TNA) is a process designed to identify the gap between what employees actually know and do, and what they should know and do in the context of an organization's stated objectives.

TNA must start with a clear articulation of the organization's operational strategy and business needs. What is the organization in business for? What is it trying to achieve? How is it going to meet its objectives? Such questions are, in turn, influenced by factors such as economic and technological change, the performance of suppliers and competitors, and the requirements of employees and shareholders. However, unless an organization is clear about what it wants to do and how it intends to get there, there is no objective basis for planning any form of development or training.

Once the organization's mission has been qualified, work can begin on assessing the training required to achieve it. This customarily involves discovering the answer to two questions:

1 Which behavioural competencies are important in performing given jobs?
2 Which competencies do employees identify as having training needs?

The answer to the first question can be found by applying the job analysis techniques described in Chapter 1: for example, critical incident techniques can be used to uncover the sort of behaviour which is key to successful job performance. At an individual level asking questions about what is important in a particular job provides clues about the relevance of certain activities and how interesting they are to the employee. This feeds directly into issues of job satisfaction and, arguably, to the form of training required to meet the need. For example, training which is designed to develop capability in a tactical sense is often applied immediately. The typically short duration of such training also means that it is the learning transfer which takes place on the return to the workplace which makes the difference.

The second question has a different emphasis and provides information on the learning priorities of the workforce. It gives an indication of readiness to learn, as, clearly, people will be resistant to training in those areas which they perceive as having a low priority. This can produce problems as it is not unusual for employees to avoid training in areas where they actually need it! Examples of this abound in most organizations, especially with regard to employees who have been performing jobs for considerable periods of time. To suggest in such circumstances that there are better ways of doing things, or that a well established approach should be modified, can be met with outright hostility. This is often not only due to inadequate appraisal procedures, which should have identified areas for improvement over the years, but also to more fundamental factors such as the organization's culture. A different culture, such as that encompassed by a learning organization, would have produced a quite different outcome. After all, employees are far less resistant to change if they perceive learning as being a continuous process in which all are involved.

In traditional TNA when employees recognize the importance of particular competencies, and buy-in to the need for development, a strong training need is identified. This makes sense from an individual standpoint and also satisfies most organizations. Yet, despite the willingness of individuals to be trained and the availability of resources, many training activities fail. Why? The following case history provides the missing part of the jigsaw.

Case study: Caroline and the computer

Caroline worked as a processing clerk in a publishing company. Many of the firm's activities, including her own, depended on the use of computer equipment. However, while Caroline knew how to use her computer for processing she did not understand how it could be applied to other activities. Deep down, she knew that she ought to know something else about computers, but she had no reason to learn.

During her annual appraisal Caroline was asked if she would like to learn how to use her computer for desktop publishing. This had been identified as a business need and Caroline was considered to be the best person to take on the extra responsibility. The thought of attending a course worried Caroline a little, but she was also excited by the thought of being able to do something new. After thinking it over carefully she volunteered for the course.

Caroline attended the course and returned to work full of new ideas. She was anxious to try out her new skills but her supervisor reminded her that she still had to complete her normal work. Her workmates were also happy to point out that she would have to practise her publishing skills in her own time as they would not take on any of her work. Caroline detected that her colleagues were jealous and that they thought that she was 'getting above herself'.

After a while, Caroline's enthusiasm died down and she concentrated on her old job. Soon she forgot most of what she had learnt. She decided that she would not volunteer for that sort of training again as it had only caused her anxiety and made her stand out from her colleagues. Her manager could not understand why she had given up and was annoyed. He decided that the business had wasted its money sending Caroline on the course.

Caroline's plight highlights a third question which needs to be asked – namely, what competencies are likely to be supported and rewarded? It is not sufficient to identify a need and provide training; the activity must be rewarded and encouraged. This extremely fundamental factor is frequently overlooked. Reward in this context does not necessarily mean money but the way in which the organization accommodates to the newly skilled employee. Are there changes to the way in which work is allocated? Has the impact on work colleagues been considered? How will work norms be changed?

In conclusion, TNA needs to be centred on individuals and organizations. Both need to know in detail about job competencies, how training needs can address business objectives and what sort of training will be mutually reinforcing. A mismatch between any of these factors will inevitably lead to training problems.

Different types of training

One of the most common forms of training is that which is performed on-the-job (OJT). This is usually associated with new employees, takes place during working hours, and is used for semi-skilled positions. Typically the training is performed by a peer or colleague and takes place at the trainee's work station. For instance, McDonalds employs a 'crew' of mostly young people who receive hands-on training from a 'buddy' – someone who has received training in how to train and is competent in the use of the staff training resources. The system has proved to be particularly effective, especially given McDonald's focus on quality and consistency, and tends to throw into doubt the views of those who consider OJT ('sitting by Nellie') to be the poor relation of the training family. Indeed OJT often extends beyond preparation, processing and manufacturing jobs; there are numerous examples in the service and public sectors.

To formally establish OJT within an organization it is important to gain the commitment and involvement of both senior and line managers. In the McDonald's example the final assessment of trainees is carried out by the restaurant manager, who is in turn checked out by an area manager. For such a system to work the process must obviously be systemized and documented and a suitable cadre of good on-the-job trainers must be available. Other issues such as whether trainers should receive special payments, and mechanisms for ensuring that training is carried out consistently, also need to be addressed.

There are numerous other forms of training apart from OJT. Some take place on-the-job and others off-the-job, and many involve groups or teams. The training environment can also vary – some training events taking place indoors and some outdoors. A brief list of the different types of training which are used for staff development is presented below:

- **Formal training**. This takes the form of a training course, often lasting a number of days, delivered by professional trainers as an in-company event or at an off-site training venue. This format follows a traditional educational model and is what most people, especially managers, consider as training.
- **Distance learning**. This type of training requires the trainee to undertake individual assignments, usually outside office hours, supported by written training materials. Depending on the form of training other learning resources such as videos, computer packages, CD-ROMS or similar may be involved.
- **Coaching**. This is a formal or informal relationship between a manager and a subordinate which is designed to give the subordinate developmental guidance. A similar relationship is 'mentoring' in which a senior manager, often from a different department, acts as an expert guide.
- **Job rotation**. This is a form of training, common in the retail sector, which works by exposing the trainee to a range of different jobs within an organization. A related activity is 'job enrichment' in which an individual's job is broadened by the inclusion of additional tasks and responsibilities.
- **Project management**. Large organizations may form cross-disciplinary project teams to address specific business problems. Frequently these have the dual purpose of not only working on a given problem, but also of exposing team members to new ideas and ways of operating.

- **Secondments**. This is a type of training which involves loaning an employee to another organization. This is not unusual for managers, professional staff and consultants and, in some instances, for production or process workers. For example, a manufacturing organization relocating to a different country may second employees from the host country to its home base.
- **Sabbaticals**. Some organizations allow employees time off to pursue personal interests or gain additional qualifications. This is perhaps the epitome of off-site training as the employee does no official work during this period. Most sabbaticals last between six and 12 months and, in some countries, they are available automatically after having worked for an employer for a given period of time.

The list could be extended to include reading, conferences, seminars and more physical activities such as outdoor training. The point is that there are many forms of training, and a formal programme should include a mixture of activities. In addition, those commissioning or delivering training need to consider the sort of activity which will most suit individual trainees. This is a question of learning style.

Learning style

People learn in different ways. The best equipped learn in a cyclical fashion in which they pass from an active 'doing' phase, through a period of observing or reflecting on their performance, to a stage concerned with linking or connecting experience to what they already know. Finally, they move into a period of deciding, or decision-making, and back into action once more. Figure 6.1 illustrates this cycle.

The doing phase is self-evidently about performing a task. From a learning perspective it is also about having an experience in a reactive or proactive sense. Reactively it might concern responding to another person – maybe a manager or a trainer – and proactively executing a personal decision. In the observing phase the learner becomes a conscious evaluator of his or her own actions, assessing what has been done and deciding whether it was done effectively, or whether there is room for improvement. The next phase, that of linking, is about placing what has happened in context. How does the learning experience connect with similar experiences? What has been learnt? Finally, during the deciding phase, a new course of action is selected from a number of alternatives. A choice is made and the learner performs another action.

The phases can be seen to fall into pairs – those which are to do with action or thinking, and those which take place at an abstract or concrete level. Interestingly, as learners, we all have distinct preferences.

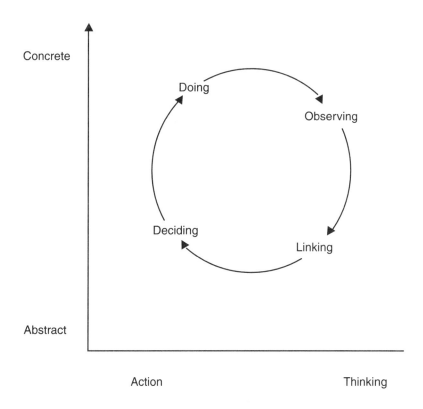

Figure 6.1   The learning cycle

Indeed, research by Peter Honey, the well known UK psychologist and management consultant, reveals some quite unexpected results. First, about 95 per cent of us do not move through the entire learning cycle in an orderly way, and actually miss out some phases completely. To be precise, approximately 35 per cent have one preference, 25 per cent two preferences and 20 per cent three preferences. The remainder have no preferences at all.

In practical terms this means that trainers must produce learning materials, or organize events, which take into account individual preferences, and encourage trainees to adopt a more holistic learning style. The most effective learning programmes force trainees to move through all four phases. In order to facilitate this type of learning many trainers find it useful to use a learning styles questionnaire in advance of a training event. There are a number available including the *Learning Styles Questionnaire* developed by Peter Honey and Alan Mumford. This is the world's most widely used measure of learning styles which classifies individuals as being activists (doers), reflectors (observers), theorists (linkers) or pragmatists (deciders). It is available in Honey and Mumford's book,

Manual of Learning Styles (Maidenhead: Peter Honey), and a shortened version is also reproduced in *Understanding How People Learn* by David Reay (London: Kogan Page). A computer-based version, which can be used to analyse the training styles of teams, can be purchased from the UK publisher Psi-Press. Contact details are provided at the end of this book.

Choosing and evaluating training

The process of selecting a training provider is the same as seeking tenders for any other form of consultancy, and guidelines are provided in Chapter 8. However, an additional step which needs to be considered is that of evaluating the impact of training. This should include an assessment of the trainer and the training format, a justification of the training itself and some of the financial considerations detailed at the beginning of this chapter. Pragmatically, organizations can evaluate training at one of four distinct levels:

- **Reaction.** This measures what the trainees or delegates think about the training. Typically this involves the completion of a course feedback form.
- **Immediate.** This assesses what the trainees or delegates have learnt. This often involves some form of continuous assessment or an end-of-course test.
- **Intermediate.** This is concerned with the effect of training on job performance. This is more difficult to assess and relies on an obvious link between what has been learnt and job content.
- **Ultimate.** This is the hardest of all to assess and involves an estimate of the effect of training on organizational performance. The ultimate criterion here is profit.

The problem is that most training is only evaluated at the first level. This is useful in that it probes the acceptability of the form of training used, but has little to say about its actual effectiveness. Measuring effectiveness requires some form of formal (immediate) assessment, preferably coupled with an intermediate-level follow-up which implies the use of formal appraisal procedures. Finally, as a matter of commonsense, all businesses should try to assess training at an organizational level, since all training activities should have obvious connections with business needs and objectives. If training cannot be reconciled at an organizational level it usually means that it is being driven by partisan interests and is not, fundamentally, in the interests of the organization as a whole.

Training checklist

- Identify business needs and objectives.
- Decide on the overall aim of the training.
- Agree aims with senior management.
- Identify groups, or individuals, requiring training.
- Evaluate different training formats.
- Use pre-event learning style questionnaires.
- Decide on method of delivery – for example, OJT, in-house, off-site.
- Consider the timing and duration of training.
- Ensure that on-site trainers are properly trained.
- Check credentials of trainer providers, if employed.
- Check that materials, resources and venue are acceptable.
- Provide trainees with a detailed course outline.
- Establish a rigorous method of evaluating outcomes.
- Follow up training with trainees after the event.

Management development

Training for managers is usually styled as 'development' but it is essentially the same as any other form of training. It differs only in that there is often more choice available and managers themselves tend to be volunteers. This is in marked contrast to OJT and skills-based training in which there is often an element of compulsion. Some of the techniques used to evaluate participants on developmental courses may also be more involved, as may the courses themselves. The aims may also differ substantially from skills-based training and be concerned with the development of 'managerial' competencies such as leadership and teambuilding. A good example is the use of outdoor training courses which are becoming increasingly popular and are aimed principally at existing managers and graduate trainees. They usually consist of a mixture of self-exploration, practical exercises conducted in groups, and detailed review sessions, the idea being to transfer the lessons learnt in an unfamiliar environment to the problems and issues encountered in the workplace.

Development centres

One of the most sophisticated forms of managerial development is the development centre (DC). This is a development event which takes place away from the workplace and in which a small number of participants complete a range of job-related exercises. These are similar to the sort of exercises used in assessment centres (see Chapter 3) and include psychometric tests, structured interviews, problem-solving tasks and group exercises. The performance of the participants (a term used in preference to 'candidate' with its overtones of selection) is monitored by trained observers.

In contrast to an assessment centre, a DC is not concerned with making final decisions about participants. Instead, the information generated is used in conjunction with appraisal ratings, on-the-job performance and individual career aspirations, to produce an individual development report. This may be concerned solely with personal development, or be used to introduce a competency framework to prepare participants for higher-level jobs. Although some elements will have been discussed during the assessment period, the report is produced after the centre and summarizes the developmental evidence gathered by the observers. Participants gain access to their own reports about two or three weeks after the DC, at which time they also receive detailed feedback from one of the observers. In addition, they will have had an opportunity to comment on the DC using feedback forms, and to express personal views which will have been taken into account during the preparation of each report. In most DCs, reports remain confidential and form part of a participant's personnel file. However, depending on the outcome of the DC, line managers will usually need to be aware of the comments as they will be involved in drawing up development plans. Such plans will usually incorporate a range of different sorts of training and details on the way in which progress will be evaluated. Individual reports generally remain valid for between 18 and 24 months.

To illustrate the way in which information is used, the results of personality questionnaires are often discussed candidly with individuals during the course of the DC. For instance, the *Myers-Briggs Type Indicator®* (MBTI®), an extremely popular personality questionnaire, often plays an important role in many centres. The MBTI is based on the work of Carl Jung and the efforts of the mother–daughter team, Katherine Briggs and Isabel Myers. Isabel Myers, in particular, spent over 30 years refining the questionnaire items which were to lead to the MBTI, and which now provide a powerful way of classifying people's behaviour. It does this by identifying preferences on the following four independent dimensions:

1 Extraverted (E)–Introverted (I)
Extraverted people prefer to deal with the outer world of people, activities and things. In a work context they like interacting with other people and seek variety and action. The introvert, in contrast, is concerned with the inner world of ideas and information. He or she likes a quiet environment, tends to concentrate on one thing at a time, and prefers to work alone.

2 Sensing (S)–Intuitive (N)
The sensing person focuses on the here-and-now and on information

from the senses. He or she uses experience to solve problems and likes to undertake practical tasks. There is also a concern with detail and a preference for a step-by-step approach. Those who are intuitive are concerned with the future, strategy and possibilities. They like to consider the overview and new ways of doing things.

3 Thinking (T)–Feeling (F)

Thinkers base their decisions on the logical analysis of situations. They tend to be firm-minded, critical, no-nonsense sort of people. At times, their decisions can appear to lack a personal element. In contrast, feeling people use values and subjective information to reach decisions. They enjoy pleasing others and promote an inclusive form of working.

4 Judging (J)–Perceiving (P)

The judging person likes a planned, organized approach to life. He or she prefers to have things settled and actively seeks structure and schedules. In meetings there may be much talk of purpose and direction, and a laser-like focus on the task in hand. On the other hand, the perceiving individual likes flexibility and spontaneity. The concern is with leaving options open and delaying decisions to allow for last-minute changes.

The result of the questionnaire is a four-letter code, or type, which is associated with a unique set of behavioural attributes and characteristics. The type description forms the starting-point for individual feedback or, when groups of people are assessed, for a discussion of team roles and ways of improving intergroup communication. An extract from a report for an 'ENTJ' is reproduced at the end of this chapter (pp 142–5). For those interested in the distribution of different types in the general UK population, a recent large-scale research project revealed the following proportions:

■ Extraversion (E): 53%   Introversion (I): 47%
■ Sensing (S): 76%   Intuition (N): 24%
■ Thinking (T): 46%   Feeling (F): 54%
■ Judging (J): 58%   Perceiving (P): 42%

These figures are supplied courtesy of Oxford Psychologists Press, and readers may care to consider the interesting result for the sensing–intuition scale. These would tend to indicate that, all other things being equal, the UK population tends towards the grounded and practical, rather than the strategic and future-oriented.

The MBTI is produced by the US publisher, Consulting Psychologists Press Inc., and is available in its European English form from Oxford Psychologists Press. Both sources provide a bureau scoring service and produce detailed reports. As with other personality measures, users are required to undergo special training. In the UK this involves attendance at a Level-B training course (see Chapter 3). Oxford Psychologists Press also distributes an extensive range of books on the use of type psychology in individual development, teambuilding, organizational change, career and relationship counselling. A particularly clear and short introduction is provided by their booklet *Introduction to Type™ in Organisations*.

Individual development

In many businesses development activities do not form part of an internal programme, and the onus for development is thrown back on to individual employees. This is especially true in the professions and, in many cases, for middle and senior managers as well. As a result, there is a requirement for individual programmes of continuing professional development (CPD).

In essence CPD is systematic, ongoing and self-oriented learning. It is ongoing, or continuing, because professionals must keep up-to-date with the latest practices; it has a professional component because it is focused on competence in a specific role; and it is developmental by virtue of being concerned with growth and career progression. Above all, it is a process which is owned by the employee and which involves a wide range of developmental activities. The last point is important because the use of CPD is often a reaction to the fact that many organizations cannot physically afford the volume of training required to keep people up-to-date, and find it difficult to tailor available training to individual learning styles.

From an organizational point of view, a management process which encourages CPD, even if it only entails greater flexibility in terms of working hours, can be seen to produce a range of valuable benefits:

1 There are usually measurable improvements in the way in which employees perform their current job, because CPD concentrates attention on the competencies required for superior performance and any areas in which additional knowledge is required.
2 It can bring into focus the potential within individual employees and lead to better informed progression management. Obviously for the employee it can also increase employability outside the organization.
3 Perhaps most importantly, it enhances the capacity to learn. In many businesses a workforce that is continually upskilling may be their only edge over the competition. At a practical level this manifests itself in a proactive approach to learning which permeates all activities.
4 Individuals, and by inference organizations, will be better placed to deal with change. The process of keeping up-to-date with new developments acts as a way of anticipating change and preparing for different work activities.

5 Because CPD raises levels of expertise it frees managerial resources and allows for greater delegation and autonomy.

The learning which constitutes CPD can take a number of different forms. Traditionally this can include attendance at a range of external courses, seminars and conferences. However, as mentioned previously, the extensive use of external training can be prohibitively expensive. In consequence, much learning is centred on work-based activities, personal activities such as voluntary work, and the informal use of books, periodicals, videos, television programmes and so forth. Of these the most powerful learning experiences are often those provided by work itself. These can include:

- **Project teams**. Many organizations encourage multidisciplinary project teams because they facilitate the exchange of information and develop teamworking skills. In a truly multidisciplinary team, members can only function by adding to their corpus of existing knowledge and by 'teaching' each other.
- **System implementation**. Any new system, whether it be concerned with production, processing, stock control, distribution, finance, quality, personnel, R&D or anything similar, requires new skills to be learnt. In addition, managers benefit from the requirement to teach other people about new operating principles or procedures.
- **Training**. As touched on above, the planning and delivery of training courses themselves encourage managers to review their existing knowledge and to develop better presentational skills. Indeed, training delivery is one of the most powerful learning situations, as trainers have the opportunity to receive direct feedback from trainees.
- **Problem resolution**. Managers or professionals who are encouraged to resolve problems which are outside their usual scope of operation acquire new knowledge and skills. For example, disciplinary or grievance procedures often require a meticulous review of the facts and a knowledge of company policies and the law.

The list could of course continue and involve secondment, job rotation and many other activities reviewed elsewhere in this chapter. However, one additional matter that does need to be addressed is: how much CPD is desirable? This will partly depend on the opportunities available to individuals and the view taken by employers, but CPD, by definition, needs to be continuous. It will also involve out-of-work activities and so is best seen as an attitude of mind rather than a rigid technique. An additional point is that it is the outcome which is paramount, not the gross amount of input. As a rule of thumb, many professional organizations recommend that CPD should take up at least 40 hours per year, spread over a range of different activities. This implies that it would not be sufficient just to attend three or four courses, but to engage in a planned mix of courses, work activities and informal learning opportunities, as well as having some mechanism for deciding what had been learnt and how it could be used in the future. This being the case, those involved in CPD often find it useful to keep a personal log detailing the duration of CPD activities, what was done and how it was done, what was learnt or achieved, and the implications. When CPD is organized by a professional body, evidence is required in the form of certificates, notes or diaries, and learners are often required to prepare short- and long-term career plans.

Mentoring

Mentoring is a good example of individual development because it provides rich opportunities for mentor and protégé alike. Whether it is used as a way of bringing on 'high flyers', or as part of an induction programme, it provides an important alternative method of career development. As a technique it is recognized by many organizations, with research by the UK-based Industrial Society indicating that about 30 per cent of firms have some form of mentoring scheme. The use of mentoring in the USA is even greater, especially in multinationals, but there is a distinct difference between what one could call the American and European models. In Europe, mentoring is seen as being mostly development- rather than progression-focused. It is not necessarily concerned with advancement and typically takes place 'off-line' – that is, it is not based on a relationship between a manager and his or her direct subordinate. In America the role of the mentor is often that of sponsor or promoter, with the explicit aim of advancing the protégé's career.

A successful mentoring relationship is one in which there is a clear understanding between mentor and protégé, which acknowledges the time and commitment required by both participants. It is essential that it is based on mutual respect, and the protégé must recognize the experience the mentor has to offer. In most cases, this implies that there will be a significant age gap between mentor and protégé, with a typical figure being at least ten to 15 years. Thus a new graduate trainee will often find that he or she has a mentor in their mid-thirties or early forties. However, that is not to say that mentoring only takes place with young employees, as it can also be effective with employees who have reached a plateau, at whatever stage in their career.

The benefits of being mentored include an easier induction into a new job or role, improved confidence in the sense that the protégé feels valued enough to receive the personal attention of a successful manager, careers advice and possible advancement (especially in US organizations), and managerial tutelage. The latter provides useful insights into how the management process operates and the unwritten rules which influence the operation and structure of the organization. Indeed, an understanding of the unwritten rules, or the tacit knowledge that is required to comprehend an organization, is often vital to successful performance within that organization's culture. For example, there may be methods of presentation which increase an individual's impact, or informal lines of communication to key decision-makers.

Case study: mentoring in practice

A multinational retailing organization decided to institute a formal mentoring programme for new entrants. This involved assigning protégés to challenging assignments under the direct supervision of personal mentors who were not their line managers. The mentors, who were all volunteers, were asked to work within a formal mentoring contract. This involved meeting the protégé for an hour at least twice a month, ensuring that the protégé kept a progress log, and maintaining an active relationship for 18 months. Mentors were also bound to keep details of their meetings with protégés confidential. In return protégés were required not to make additional demands on the mentor's time or to use the mentor's authority without permission.

In operation the mentoring programme involved 40 mentoring pairs, with many mentors and protégés being involved in the same projects but at different levels. When relationships had been established, mentors were also seen to be introducing protégés to a broad range of organizational functions and encouraging their attendance at formal and informal management meetings. Feedback logs revealed that mentors were directing protégés towards useful sources of information and contacts and encouraging a critical debate about what had been learnt and its value to the organization.

The programme included an evaluation system based on the use of feedback questionnaires and an annual workshop at which all the protégés met. This allowed protégés to comment on the mentoring process and to suggest changes and improvements. Mentors also met in a formal session to review progress. An evaluation of the programme revealed that it had increased motivation and reduced leaver rates, and that mentors considered their role to be essential to the development of organizational talent. Protégés reported that they had developed new skills (especially in problem-solving), had a greater awareness and understanding of the organization, felt that they were being actively supported and encouraged, and felt a greater commitment to the company's objectives.

Note: Traditionally, mentoring relationships involve mentors and protégés from the same organization. However, this is not always the case, as mentoring can take place when protégés are seconded to other organizations, or via the services of consultancies who specialize in external mentoring relationships.

From the mentor's perspective the role of expert coach can increase job satisfaction and stimulate a fresh look at the organization. There is also satisfaction to be gained from helping a colleague, and often lessons to be learnt from someone who may have a more recent knowledge of the latest managerial practices. In addition, the mentor will often benefit from increased recognition, especially if he or she is perceived as someone with a keen eye for talent. In short, the mentor, as part of the organizational apparatus, will smooth the path of induction, improve motivation and morale (and reduce drop-out rates), contribute to a more stable working environment and, more often than not, help develop future leaders.

However, these benefits will only flow if mentors are carefully chosen. The prime requirements are for action-oriented individuals who have an established record of developing other people, plus an interest in seeing other subordinates advance. All this should be backed up with a range of effective managerial skills, a deep understanding of the organization's culture, a good network of contacts and sufficient time to devote to the relationship. This can be quite a tall order. Finally, particular care needs to be taken in matching mentor and protégé, not just with regard to the issue of trust and the capabilities of mentors and protégés, but at the level of gender. Unfortunately, there are often difficulties with mixed-gender mentoring pairs as a result of the power relationship, especially with male mentors and female protégés, quite apart from the sexual innuendo which can arise.

An excellent introduction to mentoring is David Clutterbuck's, *Everyone Needs a Mentor* (London: IPD), which is part of the Institute of Personnel and Development development skills series.

Management development checklist

- Promote 'learning' as a legitimate managerial competence.
- Encourage everyone to accept responsibility for their own careers.
- Discourage the view that 'development' and 'promotion' are synonymous.
- Concentrate on individual development within the organizational umbrella.
- Consider 'off-site' competency-based training – for example, outdoor events.
- Explore the role of developing focused assessments – for example, development centres.
- Check the quality of delivery and process (see training checklist).
- Use specialist questionnaires and assessments – for example, MBTI®.
- Encourage CPD initiatives in professional and managerial staff.
- Ensure that CPD involves a range of developmental activities.

■ Consider the introduction of a mentoring programme.
■ Use feedback questionnaires and workshops to evaluate initiatives.

Using training and development techniques

In many organizations training and development plays something of a Cinderella role. Yet it is an area in which enormous improvements can be made in work performance and staff motivation. Indeed, in highly competitive situations, which are usually characterized by organizations which offer similar products or services, superior training or 'organizational learning' is one of the few activities which can provide an edge on the competition.

To be effective any form of learning needs to be directly linked to the organization's requirements. It is not sufficient to use it as a means of 'reward' (the corporate 'jolly') or as a way of providing an illusion of upskilling. It must be rooted in a thorough training needs analysis which is coupled to an integrated series of training events. For organizations unfamiliar with formal training analyses professional support is essential; in addition, although learning style questionnaires, for example, are openly available, organizations are well advised to obtain help in their use. Access to developmental personality measures such as the MBTI® will most certainly be restricted to suitably trained psychologists or HR professionals.

Some of the more complex development strategies such as development centres and mentoring programmes also require specialist input. In particular, development centres, while they should always include line managers from the parent organization, are multifaceted learning processes with a high degree of 'psychological' content. Because of this, they should routinely involve a business psychologist. To be successful a mentoring programme may also require support in the early days, and the mentors themselves will probably require some form of basic counselling training.

In summary, training activities increase the intellectual capital and corporate resilience of organizations. They should be applied in a thoughtful and strategic way across the entire organization as there is little point in developing managers while neglecting other employees, or vice versa.

Example MBTI® development narrative*

ENTJ

Extraverted Intuition with Thinking

People with ENTJ preferences use their Thinking preference to run as much of the world as may be theirs to run. They enjoy executive action and long-range planning. Reliance on Thinking makes them logical, analytical, objectively critical, and not likely to be convinced by anything but reasoning. They tend to focus on the ideas, not the people behind the ideas.

They like to think ahead, organise plans, situations, and operations related to a project, and make a systematic effort to reach objectives on schedule. They have little patience with confusion or inefficiency, and can be tough when the situation calls for toughness.

They think conduct should be ruled by logic, and govern their behaviour accordingly. They live by a definite set of rules that embody their basic judgements about the world. Any change in their ways requires a deliberate change in their rules.

They are mainly interested in seeing the possibilities beyond the present, obvious, or unknown. Intuition heightens their intellectual interest, curiosity for new ideas, tolerance for theory, and taste for complex problems.

ENTJs are seldom content in jobs that make no demand upon their Intuition. They are stimulated by problems and are often found in executive jobs where they can find and implement new solutions. Because their interest is in the big picture, they may overlook the importance of certain details. Since ENTJs tend to team up with like-minded people who may also underestimate the realities of a situation, they usually need a person around with good common sense to bring up overlooked facts and take care of important details.

Like other decisive types, ENTJs run the risk of deciding too quickly before they have fully examined the situation. They need to stop and listen to the other person's viewpoint, especially with people who are not in a position to talk back. This is seldom easy for them, but if they do not take time to understand, they may judge too quickly, without enough facts or enough regard for what other people think or feel.

ENTJs may need to work at taking Feeling values into account. Relying so much on their logical approach, they may overlook Feeling values – what they care about and what other people care about. If Feeling values are ignored too much, they may build up pressure and find expression in inappropriate ways. Although ENTJs are naturally good at seeing what is illogical and inconsistent, they may need to develop the art of appreciation. One positive way to exercise their Feeling preference is through appreciation of other people's merits and ideas. ENTJs who learn to make it a rule to mention what they like, not merely what needs correcting, find the results worthwhile both in their work and in their private lives.

---

* MBTI® and Myers-Briggs Type Indicator are registered UK and US trade marks of Consulting Psychologists Press Inc. Oxford Psychologists Press Ltd is the exclusive licensee of the trade marks in the UK. These extracts are reproduced by permission of the UK licensee.

ENTJs are logical, organised, structured, objective, and decisive about what they view as conceptually valid.

Contributions to an Organization
- Develop well thought-out plans
- Provide structure to the organisation
- Design strategies which work toward broad goals
- Take charge quickly
- Deal directly with problems caused by confusion and inefficiency

Leadership Style
- Take an action-oriented energetic approach
- Provide long-range vision to the organisation
- Manage directly and are tough when necessary
- Enjoy complex problems
- Run as much of the organisation as possible

Preferred Work Environment
- Contains results-oriented, independent people focused on solving complex problems
- Goal-oriented
- Efficient systems and people
- Challenging
- Rewards decisiveness
- Includes tough-minded people
- Structured

Potential Pitfalls
- May overlook people's needs in their focus on the task
- May overlook practical considerations and constraints
- May decide too quickly and appear impatient and domineering
- May ignore and suppress their own feelings

Suggestions for Development
- May need to factor in the human element and appreciate others' contributions
- May need to check the practical, personal, and situational resources available before plunging ahead
- May need to take time to reflect and consider all sides before deciding
- May need to learn to identify and value feelings

Your order of preferences

Your four-letter type also stands for a complex set of dynamic relationships. Every person likes some of the preferences, or functions, better than others. In fact, it is possible to predict the order with which any individual will develop and prefer using the functions.

As an ENTJ, your order is:

1 Thinking
2 Intuition
3 Sensing
4 Feeling

Thinking is your No. 1, or dominant function. The strengths of dominant Thinking are to:

- Be good at analysis
- Find flaws in advance
- Hold consistently to a policy
- Weigh "the law and the evidence"
- Stand firm against opposition

The potential pitfalls and suggestions for development are also related to your order of preferences in that the pitfalls may be the result of undeveloped preferences.

Your Problem Solving Style

When trying to solve problems, your MBTI preferences can be used to help guide the process. Although it seems straightforward, this process can actually be difficult to fully implement, because people have a tendency to skip over those parts of a problem-solving process that require them to use their less preferred functions. Decisions are usually made by emphasising your dominant function (No. 1) and by ignoring your least preferred function (No. 4). A better decision is likely to result if all of the preferences are used. Until you master this process, it might be wise to consult others of opposite preferences when making important decisions, or pay particular attention to your less preferred functions.

When solving a problem or making a decision, you are most likely to start with your dominant function, Thinking, by asking:

- What are the pros and cons of each possibility?
- What are the logical consequences of each possibility?
- What are the pleasant and unpleasant outcomes of each?
- What is the consequence of not acting?

You may then proceed to your No. 2 function, Intuition, and ask:

- What are the possibilities?
- What other ways are there for solving this problem?
- What do the data imply?
- What are the implications beyond the facts?
- What is the problem analogous to?

You are not as likely to ask questions related to your No. 3 function, Sensing, such as:

- What are the facts?
- What exactly is the situation?
- What has been done?
- What am I and others doing?
- How would an outsider look at this situation?

You are least likely to ask questions related to your No. 4 function, Feeling, such as:

- How much do I care about what I gain or lose in each alternative?

■ What are the values involved for each possibility?
■ How will the people concerned react to the outcome?
■ Will the outcome contribute to individual or group harmony?

Finally, it is important to use Perceiving (P) in each step to ensure openness to all aspects of the problem; use Judging (J) to set a timetable for moving on to the next step of the process; use Introversion (I) to reflect at each step along the way; and use Extraversion (E) to discuss each step and to implement your plan.

Further information

Bee, F. and Bee, R. (1994), *Training Needs Analysis and Evaluation*, London: IPD.

Lee, G. (1994), *Development Centres: Raising the Potential of your Employees Through Assessment and Development*, Maidenhead: McGraw-Hill.

Mumford, A. (1988), *Developing Top Managers*, Aldershot: Gower.

Peel, M. (1992), *Career Development and Planning: A Guide for Managers, Trainers and Personnel Staff,* Maidenhead: McGraw-Hill.

Managing Stress and Workplace Counselling

Overview

Stress has been one of the most important health issues of recent years. It is also set to be a major influence on work performance in the twenty-first century as technology becomes ever more sophisticated and the workforce takes on more demanding jobs. Indeed, as a result of such factors and others such as the fear of redundancy and the increasingly competitive nature of the workplace, stress-related problems now cost the UK in excess of £11 billion per year.

This chapter looks at the nature of stress and how it can be managed. The positive side of stress is explored and, as the energy generated by stress can be channelled to meet new business needs, techniques are described for using tension to motivate the workforce. This is followed by a discussion of workplace counselling and the counselling industry particularly in terms of their contribution to employee assistance and outplacement programmes. These help to deal with the principal causes of absenteeism – the 80 million working days per year which are lost to stress, drink, drugs and workplace bullying – and the disruption brought about by 'downsizing' and redundancy.

Finally, a special section deals with the assessment and counselling issues which relate to international workers, focusing in particular on the need to select and support employees who take long-term foreign assignments. This is a form of working that is becoming increasingly common among executives and professional staff employed by multinationals operating in the communications, financial and manufacturing sectors.

What is stress?

We all know how it feels to be stressed. However, many people do not realize that stress itself is neither 'good' nor 'bad', and that its effect depends entirely on what you are trying to achieve. Stress itself is simply the result of an action which places physical or psychological demands on a person and, in fact, a certain amount of the right sort of stress, sometimes called 'eustress', is important for optimal performance. This may explain why many people work more effectively when they are close to a deadline. The approach of the deadline leads to a physiological reaction which stimulates performance, although if that person is already operating at their full potential the increased burden would have the opposite effect and performance would decline. In this case, he or she really would be 'stressed'. The nature of stress is therefore double-edged, and if one produces a graph of stress against performance the result is U-shaped (see Figure 7.1)

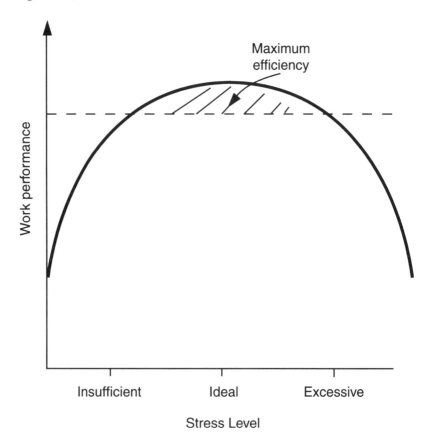

Figure 7.1 The effects of stress on performance

The role of the manager is to be aware of the relationship between stress and performance and to ensure that people experience the 'right' amount of stress. Naturally the amount which leads to optimal performance (maximum efficiency) varies from person to person, but if it can be managed it will ensure that stress stimulates rather than hinders work activity.

Sources of stress

Organizations need to understand that, if stress is unchecked, it can lead to expensive mistakes and, in some work environments, an increase in accidents. Important clients or customers can be lost through poor work behaviour or indecision and, when staff are stressed for long periods, key personnel may resign. This can damage the motivation and morale of the remaining workforce and leave gaps which are difficult to fill.

Managers must understand that people's ability to deal with pressure and the stress that it causes is not limitless and that potential stressors, or sources of work 'distress', need to be identified and quantified. A stress management strategy can then be put in place and help address the 'duty of care' incumbent on all employers. A thorough 'stress' audit also needs to take into account stressors which are external to the workplace such as the death of a spouse or close family member, divorce and marital separation, illness, change in financial circumstances and so forth.

Some of the major work stressors are as follows:

- **Excessive workload**. A period of continuous and excessive work can lead to emotional and physical burn-out. Even those individuals who appear to thrive on 'hard work' may well start to show a number of negative reactions (see Table 7.1 on p. 151).
- **Delayering**. Flatter organizations require employees, and certainly managers, to assume a wider range of roles and responsibilities. When this is coupled with inadequate training, or no training at all, significant stress can ensue.
- **Uncertainty**. The sheer pace of organizational change can lead to conflict and uncertainty. Many employees react badly to change, especially if organizations make no attempt to explain what is happening.
- **Fear**. Many people are frightened to admit that they feel stressed. This can, in itself, promote further feelings of stress and be exacerbated if organizations are going through a period of restructuring or downsizing. Who is going to admit to a stress problem when redundancies are planned?
- **Presenteeism**. Employees often feel that they must work for long periods of time. For example, in the UK more people work over 46 hours per week than in any other EU country. This is linked to a perception that it is necessary to be seen as working long hours in order to justify a decent salary.
- **Ambiguous targets**. A significant cause of stress is an uncertainty over what is required in terms of output. Often this is coupled with poor

management support and 'new' working practices. For example, those that work from home or who 'hot desk' – work for organizations in which work stations are allocated on a 'first come, first served' basis – often worry that they are not being sufficiently productive.

■ **Short contracts.** Many employees in the public and private sectors periodically have to tender for their own jobs. This increases levels of uncertainty, especially with regard to financial security, and introduces an additional element of competition into the employment situation.

■ **Workplace bullying.** This is an often unrecognized stressor which exists in many workplaces. Yet any co-worker behaviour which undermines a person's confidence or authority, and adversely affects feelings of self-worth and adequacy, can be a significant cause of stress – see the case study on pp 159–60.

■ **Personality clashes.** Difficult relationships and a lack of 'chemistry' with subordinates, colleagues or managers can all be stressful. They can lead to feelings of isolation and a lack of social support.

■ **Motivational blocks.** All the factors mentioned in Chapter 4 such as lack of power, status, independence, opportunity, poor promotion prospects and little intellectual challenge can lead to frustration and stress. Interestingly, boredom, or too little to do, can be just as stressful as too much work.

In practice, a number of these stressors may interact and add to the individual's overall stress levels. However, there are other factors which help to mediate the effects of stress which should also be recognized in any complete stress review. For instance, some people because of their genetic make-up are more resistant to stress than others. Additionally, factors such as a good sense of humour, a balanced diet, sufficient sleep and relaxation, financial security, a stable home life and an understanding of stress itself can lead to fewer stress-related problems. Simply understanding stress can be especially effective if it is linked to a stress management programme in which employees are taught to recognize their reactions to stress. Such programmes often concentrate on the following questions:

■ How do you feel when you are stressed?
■ How does this show itself?
■ How do you interpret what you feel?
■ How do you deal with stress?
■ How does it affect those close to you?
■ How do they respond to your stress?

To take just one of these questions – that of the way in which stress shows itself – work can then take place on identifying and responding to the signs of stress before they herald a full-blown problem. A representative list of signs is presented in Table 7.1.

Table 7.1   Signs of stress

Behaviour

- Working longer and longer hours
- Not managing time properly
- Becoming disorganized and forgetful
- Bringing work home more often
- Being unable to delegate
- Blaming others for work problems
- Procrastinating or avoiding issues
- Finding little time for enjoyment
- Losing touch with friends and relatives
- Needing stimulants, drugs, drink and so on

Feelings

- Anxiety or panic attacks
- Low energy and fatigue
- Becoming short-tempered
- Feeling down and miserable
- Lack of self-confidence
- Agitation and jumpiness
- Feeling out of control
- Worrying about insignificant problems
- Feeling emotional and tearful
- Being unable to concentrate

Sensations

- Headaches and backache
- Disrupted or poor-quality sleep
- Tension and muscle cramps
- Digestive problems
- Coronary or heart problems
- More frequent coughs and colds
- Eating more or less than usual
- Reduced or enhanced need for sex
- Nervous ticks and twitches
- Aggravated asthma, psoriasis, eczema and so on

Stress management schemes are usually delivered through employee assistance programmes or short courses. They involve organizational audits, which take place in advance of any intervention, and assessments of the stress experienced by individual employees. Emphasis is then placed on methods of coping with stress and the executive management of stress in the workplace.

Measuring stress

A number of medical and psychological measures can be used to assess stress. For instance, Thomas Holmes and Richard Rahe of the University of Washington Medical School have produced a way of evaluating personal stress called the *Social Readjustment Rating Scale*. This is reproduced in many books and manuals – for example, in Richard Gross's *Psychology: The Science and Mind of Behaviour* (London: Hodder & Stoughton), and provides a broad-brush measure of stressors, including many which are work-related. Another measure, the *Hanson Scale of Stress Resistance*, looks at the issue of stress resistance – for example, the balance between a healthy lifestyle and a stable home, and the wrong job and unrealistic work goals. This can be found in Peter Hanson's book *The Joy of Stress*, published by Andrews and McMeel.

At a psychometric level there are assessments for what are termed Type A and Type B behaviour. Those with a Type A behaviour pattern are competitive, achieving, aggressive, impatient and restless. They are often under pressure of time or responsibility and are frequently 'workaholics'. In contrast, Type Bs are more relaxed, unpressured and able to work without becoming agitated. Unsurprisingly, there is a link between Type As and work-related stress, and also with coronary heart disease. Further details can be found in a book by the originators of the concept, Friedman and Rosenman, entitled *Type A Behavior and your Heart* (New York: Knopf). The *Jenkin's Activity Survey* also assesses Type A behaviour. This is available from The Psychological Corporation.

More recently, the UK publishers, ASE, have produced a specialist stress assessment called the *Occupational Stress Indicator* (OSI). This is a paper-and-pencil or computer-administered questionnaire which aims to provide the answers to four key questions:

- What stress effects are currently being experienced?
- In what ways does the behaviour of the individual (or group) increase the stressful nature of the demands being made?
- What aspects of the organization and the roles within it are perceived as stressors?
- What strategies are currently being used to cope and how effective are these?

The OSI can be used to produce a computer-generated report. An example is provided at the end of this chapter (pp 166–9).

Finally, a number of mainstream personality questionnaires, like the *Occupational Personality Questionnaire®*, can be used to generate information on potential stressors and preferred coping styles. However, it should be recognized that personality questionnaires are not clinical instruments and it is unwise to draw conclusions about someone's state of mind or stability from them.

Managing stress

The first thing to understand is that stress is not a disease and that management methods must reflect the fact that it is a perfectly natural reaction to many circumstances. Nevertheless, it does need to be taken seriously, and employees must be provided with the means of controlling their own stress levels. This means that the organization should become aware of its own 'stress map' – those structural factors that can cause stress – and also use the available technology, such as the questionnaires mentioned or interview-based stress assessments, to determine individual stress levels.

The audit approach, which is currently very popular, involves a psychologist undertaking an examination of a business in order to give insights into potential problem areas. The emphasis is on avoiding blame and on identifying what can be done to reduce negative stress while at the same time increasing 'eustress'. In this way, the process is not solely concerned with the harmful nature of stress but with its potential positive effects on productivity and efficiency. The philosophy generally emphasizes that 'prevention is better than cure' and that work and non-work stress are cumulative. The implication of the last point is that, if stress is to be positive, employers must ensure, as far as possible, that home and work are in balance – and that the process of assessing stress within the organization is not in itself stressful!

The output of an audit should be a list of potential problems and solutions. At an individual level, the total 'weight' of stressors needs to be established and a range of possible coping mechanisms identified. For example, an organizational audit might establish that employees feel that they have insufficient time to make important decisions. The solution for the organization might be to commission a series of time management courses; the immediate answer for the individual might be a scheduled time for planning and decision-making each day. Likewise, if employees report that they feel mentally exhausted, the organization can insist that rest breaks are taken or provide a way of moderating tiredness by providing exercise equipment.

In short, organizational stress management is about creating the conditions in which employees can perform to their full potential. This involves supporting everyone within an organization, even those who seem to perform better when they are under considerable stress. Indeed such people – and many audits suggest that about 15 per cent of employees are stimulated by excessive pressure – must be very carefully managed, since stress is cumulative and high performers may be unaware of its corrosive effects. For the remaining employees an active stress management programme can yield higher levels of productivity and greater work satisfaction. However, any programme must be followed up so that managers always have an up-to-date picture of the stress issues within the organization. In particular, a close watch should be kept on the development of individual coping strategies such as planning, physical fitness, mental fitness (new problem-solving methods), assertiveness, social support and relaxation.

The following case study gives an idea of how a stress problem was turned into a positive employment experience.

Case study: James the perfectionist

James had been having problems coping at work. His manager had been trying to increase his workload and to encourage him to try some newer working methods. This had made James feel pressurized and had led to a decrease in performance. Specifically, he complained that he did not have enough time to learn anything new and that the increased load was affecting the quality of his existing work.

James was suffering from tension headaches and a loss of appetite. At times he also felt that his concentration was suffering, and he had noticed that he had started to forget things. These symptoms had begun to unsettle James and affect his confidence. When asked, he would say that his manager was being unrealistic and did not understand the real demands of his job – in particular, that to do his job well he had to have a keen eye for detail.

An organizational audit had shown that a number of employees – not just James – were feeling marginalized by new working methods, especially by the introduction of a new IT system which employees had been asked to implement without sufficient training. At a personal level a stress questionnaire confirmed that James no longer felt in control of his work and that 'impossible' targets had been set. The questionnaire confirmed that he had problems with relaxing and winding-down, which had now started to spill over into his home life.

James's manager had initially interpreted his problems as being due to his inflexibility and inability to cope with new technology. However, once the audit and the results of the stress questionnaire were known, he realized that the changes had been introduced too quickly and without sufficient warning. Remedial action for all staff was taken to deal with the

IT issue, and an action plan, dealing with working practices and time management, was drawn up for James. The audit also confirmed that James was correct to be concerned with issues of quality. In fact, his concern for quality was reinterpreted as being of considerable benefit to the organization and he was offered the opportunity to attend an auditor's course. This subsequently allowed him to become part of the organization's quality management team.

The above case study illustrates how James's stress problems were recognized and remedied. The 'creative tension' caused by his concern for quality was identified and used to enrich his job, highlighting the fact that many stressors can have either a positive or negative effect. Happily for James, his perfectionist nature was perceived as an asset to the organization. More generally, the results of stress audits should be treated carefully. The initial reaction is to try to remove the stressors which are revealed but, in practice, a better strategy is to analyse the context in which stress is occurring and to try to modify the stressors constructively so that the energy which is inherent in the stress reaction can be channelled into more productive activities. In this way, something which had become a stressor for James – that is, not being able to manage the details – was transformed into a positive experience by an attitudinal shift on the part of the organization.

The powerful way in which attitudes can switch negative stress to positive is one of the keys to stress management. However, this can only happen if organizations have objective information with which to work and also acknowledge that there are some situations which must be dealt with immediately. Employees have a right to be protected from sources of stress which arise from employer negligence, especially those which bear on health and safety, or are due to psychological factors, such as victimization. Furthermore, it is not sufficient to claim, for example, that someone *wants* to work excessive hours. Even in countries like Japan, where this attitude is rooted at a deeply cultural level, compensation claims for *karoshi,* or death from overwork, are becoming more common.

Stress management checklist

■ Familiarize yourself with relevant health and safety legislation.
■ Learn to recognize the signs of stress in others.
■ Have stress management training, if appropriate.

With professional assistance:

■ Undertake or commission an organizational stress audit.
■ Use questionnaires/interviews to assess individual stress levels.

- Analyse results and isolate negative and positive stressors.
- Consider the organizational context of stressors.
- Ask individuals about sources of non-work stress.
- Develop long-term solutions, not quick fixes.
- Produce individual stress management programmes.
- Ensure access to appropriate resources – for example, books, videos, training.
- Periodically review progress and re-audit.

Workplace counselling

Counselling for stress and other work-related problems is now common-place. Indeed, many organizations retain the services of counsellors, buy in to employee assistance programmes, or have specially trained members of staff who can deliver counselling services on demand. Why? In many ways, the reasons are quite complex, but perhaps the most persuasive argument is that counselling can directly influence profit. Benefits are quantifiable and include a reduction in accidents and absenteeism, increased productivity and less litigation. In addition, employees feel valued and the working environment is perceived as being supportive and non-threatening. At a general level the provision of counselling services acts as a signal that the organization cares about its employees and oper-ates in an ethical manner – in other words, that it has accepted a social responsibility for its employees and has moved beyond a concern only for maximizing its profits.

In those organizations in which trained staff take on the counselling role problems are often tackled during annual appraisals. This is the best time to deal with counselling issues as solutions can be incorporated into personal development plans. Follow-ups can then focus on progress and the facilitation of the outcomes agreed at the appraisal. External counsel-lors operate in a different way and are drawn into organizations in a consultative capacity, possibly with the aim of providing answers to immediate problems or achieving some longer-lasting change. Obviously the nature of the intervention depends on the organization in question and whether it is concerned with enhancing its welfare provision or some other objective.

Counselling techniques

All counselling depends on well developed interpersonal skills coupled with a coherent process of problem management. Importantly, while some of the skills are part of the managerial repertoire, others often need to be developed. For this reason alone, 'home grown' counsellors must be properly trained. Counselling training programmes often concentrate on the following skills:

- **Listening**. Many people are good at telling others what to do but lack practice in actively listening. Listening to what somebody is saying, or not saying, can reveal a great deal about what that person thinks, feels and knows. The related skill of attending, or demonstrating attention through maintaining eye contact, nodding or verbally acknowledging through saying 'hmm' or 'yes', is equally important.
- **Questioning**. There are many different types of questions and they must be used in the correct combination. Frequently, this involves starting with an open question or one that cannot be answered with a simple 'yes' or 'no', and then focusing the discussion with carefully chosen closed questions.
- **Reflecting**. This is a form of clarification or paraphrase which involves repeating what has been said. It acts as a way of showing understanding and moves the conversation forward. Additionally, it demonstrates an open-minded response to the conversation, as the counsellor does not make any value judgements.
- **Silence**. Many people, and especially new counsellors, feel uncomfortable with silence. However, it is an important part of the counselling process as it allows people to think through what they want to say, or what has been said.
- **Self-disclosure**. This is a statement of personal information about the counsellor, which is sometimes necessary to get the conversation going, especially if sensitive matters are to be discussed. It also helps to establish the counsellor as an approachable, genuine and empathetic person.
- **Giving advice**. At times it is appropriate to provide a person with a plan of action or some advice based on a particular source of information. The intention is to guide or direct the other person's behaviour in order to bring about a change in behaviour. In reality, most work-based counselling programmes involve the use of advice, with the counsellor and client agreeing a course of action.
- **Interpretation**. This is an account of what has been said in terms of cause and effect. It is used by the counsellor to explain what has happened and to help the other person understand himself or herself differently. The danger is that it is very easy to overinterpret what has been said, and so counsellors need to be aware of influencing others on the basis of incomplete information.

There are other skills that could be mentioned such as summarizing, which is similar to reflecting but, like different forms of questioning, these are usually extensively covered in training programmes. Interestingly, research conducted by the author with crisis counsellors has shown that training influences the use of reflections and silence, and that those with only basic training rely too heavily on questioning and advising. These findings make the point that training is required if counsellors are to make the best use of the complete range of responding skills.

All the skills mentioned need to be used within a well understood problem management process. One of the most straightforward was devised by the counselling psychologist Richard Nelson-Jones and is known by the acronym DOSIE. This five-stage model, which allows for collaborative problem-solving, is outlined below:

- **Stage 1 – Describe.** This is concerned with building an alliance between the counsellor and client and identifying problem areas.
- **Stage 2 – Operationalize.** In this stage the client is encouraged to acknowledge problems and develop new insights.
- **Stage 3 – Set Goals.** The counsellor and client negotiate goals and the interventions required to achieve them.
- **Stage 4 – Intervene.** The client works on problem areas and receives support from the counsellor.
- **Stage 5 – Exit.** The counselling process is reviewed and advice is given on consolidating self-help skills.

There are many more elaborate models but this has the virtue of being logical and easy to remember. When taken as the benchmark for a counselling programme it also allows employers to check the sometimes esoteric offerings of counselling providers. For example, do they impose solutions or encourage employees to recognize problems and produce their own answers? Is the 'exit' stage an integral part of the process or are employees left to review their progress alone?

Selecting a counselling provider

Before making any decisions about counselling, managers must decide what they want from the service. As already mentioned, this involves such considerations as the relative merits of in-house or outsourced counselling, but also answering questions such as:

- What do the stakeholders (senior managers, line managers, employees) expect?
- Can the expectations of all these people be reconciled and delivered?
- Is it possible to add counselling to the existing welfare operation?
- What are the practical and financial constraints on offering a counselling service?

With regard to the last question do you want to provide face-to-face counselling or a telephone-based service? Do you want to have 24-hour

365-day per year access or will limited cover be sufficient? Is the service to be available to all employees or just particular grades?

The next step is to identify a list of organizations offering the services or training you seek. Important considerations here are to look for those with experience in dealing with the counselling problems faced by your organization, and the ability to respond in the timeframe required. In the UK employers are advised to compile a shortlist from counselling organizations which employ members of the British Psychological Society (BPS) who are also chartered occupational (business), counselling or clinical psychologists. The British Association for Counselling (BAC) also maintains a list of accredited professionals. In other countries the first point of contact should also be the professional body for psychologists or counsellors.

When three or four firms have been contacted, arrange meetings and ask them to submit proposals. If you also insist on presentations it will give you an opportunity to see whether you can work with them and if they understand your needs. Make sure that the firm is large enough to cope with your requirements or, conversely, check whether it is too high-powered for what you need. If you wish to set up your own service ensure that the training provider will help you launch your programme and will be on hand to support your counsellors during the early days.

Once you have agreed the basic employee assistance programme make sure that you receive written confirmation of costs and service provision. Ensure that you have full details of consultancy, training and counselling delivery. In particular, what is the actual cost of face-to-face counselling? Is a telephone hotline included? Is there a fixed yearly fee or are counsellors charged on a usage basis? How will the counselling provider promote the service? Do they have appropriate insurance cover for general liability and malpractice? And so on.

Case study: An employee assistance programme

After a confidential survey a multinational manufacturing company became concerned about the number of employees reporting drink, drug, financial and other potentially serious problems. Evidence from line managers also confirmed that productivity was being undermined by a range of personal and work-related problems, with reports of bullying and victimization being of particular worry. Alarmingly, the survey revealed that 20 per cent of employees reported being bullied in the previous year.

The organization called in a firm, specializing in workplace counselling, to advise on the provision of a counselling service. After discussions with the consultants, who had direct experience in dealing with the issues raised, the company decided to create an in-house employee assistance programme (EAP). This was to be staffed by counsellors provided by the consultancy and a number of specially trained line managers. The EAP was designed to operate in a face-to-face manner during the working day and to provide a telephone service out of hours. It was governed by four key principles:

- **Free.** It was free to all employees, including their immediate family.
- **Confidential.** All the information provided during counselling sessions was confidential.
- **Voluntary.** Use of the service was at the employee's discretion.
- **Brief intervention.** All employees were entitled to up to ten hours of counselling per year.

The mission was to address the serious mental, emotional and physical distress reported by a significant proportion of employees.

The anti-harassment part of the programme was supported by a well publicized statement made by the Board of Directors which emphasized that there would be an immediate investigation of all reports of bullying, backed by the swift use of grievance and disciplinary procedures. On a practical level, those who were the subject of bullying were advised to work through a four-point plan culminating in a report to their manager and the union representative. This involved:

1 telling the bully to stop
2 keeping a diary of bullying incidents
3 writing to the bully each time an incident occurred, and keeping copies of all communications
4 discussing bullying incidents with colleagues in order to discover the extent of the bully's activities.

Those reporting bullying incidents also received continuous support through the counselling programme.

A later survey indicated that the new approach had significantly reduced reports of workplace bullying. Counsellors were able to provide assistance to a number of employees, including two senior executives with drink-related problems, and to support a larger group whose work performance was suffering as a consequence of the breakdown of personal relationships. Other issues addressed included emotional, health and legal problems, as well as matters concerning equal opportunities, productivity and personality 'clashes'.

Note: Experts report that bullying takes place in every type of organization and that it is a significant cause of workplace stress. If victims are bullied so badly that they become ill – and figures suggest that this may be the case in up to 70 per cent of incidents – employees have positive grounds for making personal injury claims.

Counselling and redundancy

Apart from dealing with ongoing problems, an established counselling service can be of particular importance when employees are made redundant. Counsellors, especially those supplied by external providers, can deliver a package of support services designed to help redundant employees make the necessary psychological adjustment to their new circumstances. In addition, a comprehensive approach will include assistance with job-hunting. A good example is the programme designed for the former British Coal which is delivered by British Coal Enterprises (BCE). This covers, as appropriate:

- coming to terms with redundancy
- researching the jobs market
- curriculum vitae preparation
- job application letters
- completing application forms
- job-hunting techniques
- interview skills training
- setting up a business
- retraining opportunities
- pre-retirement planning.

The BCE package has been so successful that it is now offered to a wide range of organizations, not just those involved in the mining industry. The provision of services by off-site consultancies is actually quite common as such organizations are perceived as being neutral by those that have been made redundant, and also by the surviving employees. This is an important consideration as large-scale redundancy programmes destabilize the workforce and often lead to a significant drop in morale and output. Managers must also recognize that, in some situations, redundancy programmes will encourage other staff to leave as well. This 'bail-out' phenomenon, based on the perception that 'I could be next', can be extremely damaging if it involves key staff or senior executives. In consequence, considerable effort must be put into supporting the remaining workforce and explaining what is happening. This aspect of redundancy planning is often overlooked as most of the effort is directed at organizing the logistics of the 'downsizing.'

All counsellors and those involved in redundancy programmes must appreciate the powerful psychological forces at work during periods of job loss. Many employees – not just those losing their jobs – will exhibit a range of reactions. Typically these will involve:

- absenteeism
- increased levels of 'sickness'

- poor timekeeping
- lack of concern for safety
- poor-quality work
- misuse of materials
- graffiti
- verbal abuse
- black humour
- pilfering and theft.

In extreme cases it is not unusual for companies to report incidents of arson or industrial espionage. Paradoxically, sometimes there is actually an increased commitment to work, or a tendency for everyone to continue as if nothing has happened but, even in this situation, there may still be a deliberate silence when managers are present or damage to 'symbols' of executive power.

Those losing their jobs will go through a predictable pattern of feelings similar to the process of bereavement. For many, the first stage is denial. This is characterized by a refusal to accept the situation, sometimes accompanied by displacement activities. Technically this is known as 'minimization' and it frequently manifests itself in a strong desire to 'escape' – say, by going on holiday or having a spending spree. Conversely, there may be a period of complete immobilization in which no actions are taken. Next comes a period of emotional reaction and anger. The 'injustice' of the situation hits home and those considered to be responsible become the focus of intense negative feelings. Once the anger has passed, many move into a period of fantasy in which they believe that they have been made redundant by mistake or that they are so indispensable that they will secure a new position immediately. Finally reality dawns and capitulation takes place. This is the lowest point in the cycle and is usually accompanied by a loss of energy and depression. From this point the only way is upwards, which can only be achieved by readjusting to personal circumstances. This requires confidence and self-esteem to be re-established, and it is also the first opportunity for new skills to be developed or training to be undertaken.

It is important to understand that people react at different speeds to events such as redundancy. Some will move through the stages described in a few weeks; others will take months or, in extreme cases, years. Whatever the time period there is no point in forcing people to take part in job-hunting or similar activities until they have finished reacting emotionally to what has happened. Outplacement programmes therefore need to be delivered over a considerable period of time and to respond to individuals when they are ready, not when it is convenient for the employer. Managers, especially those with a personnel or HR function, must also be prepared to be on the receiving end of considerable anger. This may require special training so that managers can cope with the pressure, and flow of raw emotion, that is inherent in the redundancy process.

Counselling checklist

- Establish the (practical) aims of the counselling service.
- Enlist support from senior management and other stakeholders.
- Make changes to organizational policies, as appropriate.
- Confirm logistical aspects such as scope, availability and staffing.
- Organize rooms for face-to-face counselling, with secure telephone lines and so on.
- Make sure that any on-site staff are properly briefed and trained.
- Thoroughly check the professional credentials of external providers.
- Establish a link with organizational welfare and grievance procedures.
- Check counsellor and organizational insurance and liability provision.
- Explain the service, and provide written details, to all employees.
- Emphasize the impartial and confidential nature of the service.
- Regularly review the use of the counselling service.

International relocation

As more organizations place staff in different countries, counselling has a growing role in international relocation. This can be an expensive business since not only does it cost as much as five times an employee's annual salary to cover one international relocation, but the opportunities for a mismatch between the employee and his or her new situation are legion.

The average length of an international assignment is between three and four years and it places a great many demands on those involved. From an organizational perspective there is the question of who is best suited to an expatriate role. Strangely this is an issue which often receives insufficient attention as, traditionally, HR departments have expended a great deal of effort devising benefit packages, and relatively little on deciding who could actually cope with working in a different country. This is a recruitment decision which is quite different to the normal process of selection as it must take into account a number of unique factors, not least the fact that a high proportion of international assignments fail because the spouse, not the direct employee, cannot adjust to a different culture. This means that, if an employee is married, selectors must consider the entire family unit when making relocation decisions – by no means an easy task as very few organizations have sufficient information to make this sort of judgement.

One solution is to perform a series of family 'interviews' in which the feelings of the spouse, and any children involved, are thoroughly explored. In addition, questionnaires such as the *Overseas Assignment Inventory* – one of the few screening tools specifically designed for this purpose, and available in the UK from PRIcoa Relocation Management Ltd – can be used to assess how well an individual will adjust to an international assignment. Nevertheless, information gained from interviews and questionnaires can only be used to try to predict whether an individual and his or her family would be able to adjust to a different culture. Further work needs to be done to ensure that the family unit is prepared for life in another country. This involves providing information on housing, shopping, banking, schooling, transport and all the other aspects of expatriate living. Ideally, this should be done well in advance of the move and be organized by someone who has first-hand experience of the country in question. Such a person also needs to be able to respond in detail to any questions asked. For example, what do you do in country X if the plumbing or electricity fails? Which schools teach courses which lead to internationally recognized qualifications? How hot and humid does it get in the summer? How cold in the winter? What is the national cuisine like? How good are the health services?

Psychologically, thought also needs to be given to 'culture shock', the term used to describe the period of emotional distress and disorientation which people feel when they first move to a different country. For many, the first few weeks or months can be extremely stressful while they come to terms with a series of new values and beliefs, which may seem to be completely alien, and discover how to do things in a culturally acceptable way. For instance, it may be difficult to reconcile personal views on law and order with a different legal system, or to understand attitudes to poverty. This period of adjustment can cause added tension within the whole family.

Needless to say, many international workers find it difficult to work effectively, especially in the early days, because business is carried out in a different way. All manner of activities, such as the way in which negotiations are conducted or the time taken to do things, may differ substantially from 'normal' practice. There may also be added pressure from the organization's home base to achieve results. The usual response to these pressures is to work longer and longer hours – a reaction which places additional strains on family members and actually inhibits cultural integration. Indeed, poor time management, and the sense of isolation it brings, is a significant contribution to spousal distress and to the failure of many relocations.

The moral is that it is incumbent on employers to ensure that employees and their families are fully briefed on what to expect, and have ongoing support in settling in and becoming established in their host country. This will smooth the adjustment of family members to their new environment and allow the employee to settle into work much more quickly. It also demonstrates a genuine commitment on the part of the parent organization to the welfare of its employees. At a more subtle level it helps to avoid friction between cultures, especially as a result of behaviour which may be perceived on either side as being inappropriate, and illustrates to nationals of the host country that a serious attempt is being made to adapt to their way of life. This is especially important for expatriates from Western countries operating within substantially different cultures.

Relocation specialists

There are a number of specialist consultancies such as PRIcoa, a subsidiary of the Prudential Insurance Company of America, who specialize in providing global relocation services. The most comprehensive deliver a package of services including:

- **Pre-departure planning** – individual assessment of employees and their families, intercultural familiarization programmes
- **Relocation** – homesale or rental if appropriate, transportation of household goods to new country
- **Destination services** – homefinding, settling in and cultural assimilation
- **On-going support** – family support, lease administration and expense management
- **Repatriation** – planning and organizing return to parent country.

Other organizations can be located on the worldwide web or by consulting reference sources such as the *Personnel Manager's Yearbook*. This carries details on a number of global relocation specialists and is updated each year. It is published by AP Information Services.

Finally, readers are reminded that international relocation is a complex mixture of selection, assessment and counselling. In light of this it is suggested that those organizations considering employees for international assignments retain the services of a specialist consultancy.

Using stress and counselling techniques

The question of who should deliver care in the workplace often promotes strong argument. Many believe that all counselling activities should be left to professionals and that line managers should play no part in the process. However, this tends to overlook the fact that, on a day-to-day basis, employees' first point of contact is their manager. That is not to say that counselling should solely be the preserve of the manager (which would generate obvious problems), rather that managers and professionals both have a role to play. The analogy is similar to training people in basic first aid so that they can recognize the signs of a heart attack. There is much that can be done before professional help arrives and, indeed, the recognition that someone is having a heart attack is the most important point of all. Similarly, it is good practice to train managers to understand the nature of stress and the physical and emotional symptoms which accompany it. The job of delivering stress audits and management programmes can then be a joint venture between an organization and stress professionals. Well trained managers can then act in a paraprofessional capacity and deliver counselling services but must always be under the supervision of a fully trained individual. In most circumstances this will be a psychologist or counsellor, and sometimes a manager who has taken an extensive course in workplace counselling. The latter is becoming more common as universities and other training providers develop specialized training courses. These are generally part-time programmes which involve study and practice over a number of years.

With regard to redundancy and outplacement counselling this is best provided by an external organization. For obvious reasons, managers would find it very difficult to actively counsel their own staff in this context and it is also very likely that their staff would resent their attempts to help. Likewise, relocation counselling is best left to an organization that specializes in such matters, not least because a genuinely objective view of the relocation candidate and his or her support network is required. However, when retaining the services of other organizations strenuous efforts must be made to match services with individual requirements and to monitor delivery. Because of this, managing the HR logistics is a crucial task: a badly organized stress management programme or an inadequate counselling service can actually make things worse.

Example OSI stress report*

Rhett O'Hara (Male)

Date of Birth: 1 Oct 1965
Date of testing: 25 Oct 1993
General Information: Sample Report

Norms used: Both sexes; General Population (N=8160)

The OSI is a questionnaire which aims to measure aspects of stress. The interpretative framework has four key factors:

- The effects of stress on Rhett at the moment.
- His individual characteristics which may help or hinder coping.
- The external factors he perceives as stressful
- The coping strategies he uses.

The Effects of Stress

Rhett appears to feel an average level of satisfaction with the nature of the work itself and with the quality of interpersonal relationships in the organization. However, he seems to have a feeling that his individual development needs are neglected and that opportunities for personal growth are lacking. Rhett also expresses dissatisfaction with the way the organization is structured (the hierarchy and flow of communication) and with the way its internal processes operate (the degree of flexibility and involvement afforded and the dynamics of supervision).

Rhett's responses suggest that his emotional well-being is within normal limits but there is a suggestion that his physical symptoms of stress are above normal levels. These may exacerbate further negative effects of stress if they are not dealt with. It is important to create time for winding down and replenishing resources for coping. Leisure activities or simply having fun can release tension. Rhett should find that regular physical exercise is a useful way of using surplus energy. Techniques for structured muscular relaxation are widely available on audio tape. Such techniques should allow Rhett to release existing tensions and prevent further build up.

Individual Characteristics

Rhett appears to have a high level of commitment to work but this is combined with a heightened pace of living. There could be an underlying tendency toward impatience and a feeling of time-urgency. This could increase Rhett's vulnerability to stress-related effects. It is important that Rhett tries to slow down occasionally and give time to the replenishment of resources by creating opportunities to relax.

Rhett indicates a perception that, although in life generally outcomes depend on individual effort, this is not the case in the work setting. He appears to believe that, at work, effort and ability do not influence outcomes. There is a feeling of being unable to affect the functioning of the organization. Rhett seems to perceive the organization as having a constraining influence on individual effort.

External Sources of Stress

Of the six external sources of stress examined by the OSI, Rhett reported that three affected him:

- Rhett's need to achieve personal and corporate success appears to be frustrated to a high degree.
- Rhett seems to feel a great deal of stress caused by his perception of the structure and process features of the organization and the general climate at work.
- The interface between home and work appear to be an area of concern for Rhett. Further exploration may be useful to highlight the exact nature of this concern.

Coping Strategies

Rhett appears to use social support as a means of enhancing his capacity to cope with life's demands. He probably finds that talking things through with colleagues is a useful way to reduce the feeling of being under stress. Even without talking things through, just the knowledge that colleagues are supportive is likely to help buffer him against the negative effects of high stress situations.

Rhett will usually confront problems and stressful situations rather than avoiding them. However, it may be that his feelings get mixed up with facts and objectivity may be reduced. It is important for Rhett to acknowledge feelings but these can be most effectively dealt with if they are separated from facts.

It would appear that Rhett does not tend to separate home and work to the same extent as most people. He should guard against losing too many opportunities to relax and unwind. These are important in helping to replenish resources and maintaining capacity for coping with the continuing demands of work.

Rhett shows a lower than average tendency to employ time-management strategies to cope with his workload. Nevertheless, at present he appears to be managing the task requirements of his job without experiencing them as particularly stressful.

Summary

It might be useful to explore the appropriateness of Rhett's coping strategies given the dissatisfaction that has been identified, together with his experience of above average levels of physical tension.

In addition his tense behavioural style may be exacerbating his perceived stress. Also his perception of a lack of control in some areas may be increasing his experience of being under pressure and making it more difficult for him to derive satisfaction from work.

Suggestions to Consider at the Individual Level

Learn to recognize and release physical tension. Consider the following techniques:

- Relaxation exercises: commercially available audio tapes give instructions in this technique. Requires approximately 20 minutes per day.
- Quick tension checks: at intervals during the day check for and consciously release tension in the mouth, shoulders, hands, feet and general posture.
- Fun: create time for leisure and enjoyment.
- Physical exercise: this should be regular and suited to individual needs.

Bear in mind that there is more to life than speed. Consciously slow down and schedule in time for the unexpected.

Consider how work time could be organized more efficiently. Time-management training may be useful.

Questions to Consider at the Organizational Level

What potential opportunities exist for individual development? Have they been utilized enough?

What improvements might be made in the way communication flows or in policies for implementing change or dealing with conflict?

Is the style of supervision appropriate for Rhett's needs?

In what way might Rhett be allowed to participate more in the decision making and objective setting?

Is there anything the organization can do to ease the interface between work and home?
Consider:

■ flexitime,
■ opportunities for working from home,
■ active discouragement of working long hours without breaks.

In what ways might characteristics of the organization be decreasing Rhett's feeling of being able to influence its functioning?

Why is there a feeling that Rhett's own efforts and performance have little influence over the results he achieves?

Further information

Addley, K. (ed.) (1997), *Occupational Stress – A Practical Approach*, Oxford: Butterworth-Heinemann.

Edelmann, R. J. (1993), *Interpersonal Conflicts at Work*, Leicester: BPS Books.

MacLennan, N. (1998), *Counselling for Managers*, Aldershot: Gower.

Nelson-Jones, R. (1989), *Practical Counselling and Helping Skills*, London: Cassell.

Consultancy Services and Business Psychologists

Overview

In this chapter we look at the services offered by psychologists and consider the role of the consultant. As you will see, business psychologists offer a wide range of services, including some not directly covered in this book. It is also true that other professionals such as HR specialists consult in overlapping areas. For example, the consultancy arms of the major accountancy firms frequently offer advice on matters such as recruitment and selection, and some even provide counselling and outplacement services. However, by employing a business psychologist you will gain a package of practice and experience that is uniquely suited to people management issues.

The consultancy market is growing rapidly, with some estimates suggesting that it is expanding by over 10 per cent per year – an impressive figure and one that is borne out in the UK by the increasing number of psychologists who specialize in providing services to the business community. It is a resource that is in demand because the costs of employing the wrong people are very high, as are the costs of maintaining inefficient teams or coping with a stressed workforce. Employers have also begun to realize that psychological interventions yield a rapid 'payback', with the initial outlay often being recovered within 12 to 18 months.

Consultancy services

The services offered by business psychologists fall into five main areas: selection and assessment, organizational development, training, work environment and human factors. The first three are covered by this book and include topics such as work profiling, psychometrics, motivation, teambuilding, training and counselling. Most general consultancies provide a portfolio of services and assessment materials designed for use in these areas, and a representative list, based on the publicity material of a number of consultancies, is presented in Table 8.1. However, some only deal in one or two areas, such as teambuilding or training, and others

Table 8.1   Consultancy services

■ Tailored job analysis and evaluation	■ Career and performance management
■ Competency framework design	■ Test design and construction
■ General recruitment and selection	■ Validation of selection procedures
■ Graduate selection and assessment	■ Attitude and motivation surveys
■ Senior executive assessment	■ 360-degree feedback and appraisal
■ Assessment/development centre design	■ Team audits and teambuilding
■ Individual career counselling	■ Employee assistance programmes

concentrate on the work environment and human factors – applications which require a particularly specialized approach.

Work environment psychologists are concerned with providing the right conditions for safe and productive working. They ensure that factors such as lighting, heating, noise and ventilation are appropriate for the work tasks being performed. At a general level they analyse the 'health' of the working environment and are often called in when employees report that the physical nature of a building is affecting their performance. In many cases this manifests itself in employees feeling fatigued because of factors such as poor natural lighting or limited access to fresh air. In extreme cases entire facilities may need to be redesigned as a consequence of what is now called 'sick building syndrome'.

In contrast, human factors – or, more correctly, ergonomics – deals with the design of work systems and equipment. This is a specialist area which includes the development of complex control systems such as those used to protect nuclear reactors or signalling for a railway. Both require a very careful analysis of the tasks involved in running a power generation plant or a transport system respectively, and an assessment of the risks involved if something goes wrong. In this way, psychologists try to protect against human failure and design fail-safe systems. Consequently, they are particularly concerned with the human–machine interface and concentrate on designing displays, controls and warning devices which are readily understood by operators – features which are important in a wide range of systems and products, from those used in manufacturing and processing to domestic appliances and aircraft cockpits.

In conclusion most business psychologists will have an understanding of the important concepts in all of the areas described, although practical experience will necessarily vary. As a result most will consult in a narrower range, the most popular being those which are directly related to selection, assessment and development.

Reasons for using consultants

It is reasonable to assume that consultants would not be used if they did not provide something that was missing in a particular organization. As a result, they are usually engaged because they provide a source of specialist knowledge, coupled with an impartial and detached viewpoint. They are also able to select from a wide range of materials and resources and to benchmark against other successful or innovative organizations. Additionally, a good consultant will want to transfer capability to the client organization and make sure that any new processes work effectively over time. Often, the consultancy option is also the most cost-effective because it is based on a limited period of intense professional help, which means that you only pay for expertise when you need it. These, and other, factors provide a powerful case for retaining the services of a consultant.

Nevertheless, a degree of caution should always be exercised when seeking professional assistance. In some cases, the link between the con-

Table 8.2   Reasons for using consultants

Likely advantages	Possible disadvantages
1 Source of independent advice	1 Close relationship with one provider
2 Expert interpretation of 'jargon'	2 Not a specialist psychologist
3 Knowledge of underlying theory	3 Poor knowledge of theory
4 Benchmark against industry standards	4 Unfamiliar with best practice
5 Use of best assessment resources	5 Rigid use of assessment materials
6 Provision of guidance on ethical issues	6 Out-of-date view of fairness issues
7 Help with transfer of expertise	7 No transfer of knowledge
8 Advice on validation and follow-up	8 Little concern with final outcome
9 Ongoing management support	9 Hidden fees and costs
10 Access to additional resources	10 Inadequate professional network

sultant and consultancy firm may not allow for a completely independent approach. For example, products designed by the firm may be used in preference to other (sometimes better) resources because they add more to the fee. This implies that the client should always expect a number of options to be presented. It may be, of course that the consultant's own materials are the most appropriate, but there should be a choice. A related problem is the rigid use of a certain approach, such as the use of particular questionnaires or tests, because these are the only ones with which the consultant is familiar. Again, a number of solutions should be on offer and the consultant must be up-to-date with the latest techniques, theories and underpinning knowledge. It should also be borne in mind that a consultant does not have to live with the outcome of an assignment and so may demonstrate less commitment than you would expect. This can be reflected in charging additional fees for follow-up work which should have been part of the original quote. Finally, be wary of a consultant who claims to be able to solve every problem; a true professional will refer you to other specialists if they are required.

Characteristics of consultants

In true psychological fashion, a review of the consultancy option would not be complete without considering the personal characteristics which make for a skilled consultant. Naturally, the dominant skills should be behavioural – particularly those concerned with communication and helping clients understand the need for various forms of change. However, there are other attributes which are prime requirements, such as a rigorous intellectual approach and sound judgement.

A number of the large American consultancy firms have spent time defining the profile of an effective consultant and recruit all their personnel against a set of 'desirable' characteristics. A typical specification might contain the following ten elements:

■ energetic with good physical health
■ self-confident and emotionally stable
■ courteous with a professional manner
■ trustworthy with high personal integrity
■ self-reliant and non-judgemental
■ analytic with strong problem-solving skills
■ intellectually competent and objective
■ skilled in interpersonal relationships
■ possessing well developed communication skills
■ self-aware and psychologically mature.

The last element is important because successful consultants must be able to respond to new situations in a clear-headed and detached way, while being mindful of their own competence in a particular area. This requires a calm and objective manner and an approach which is not coloured by illogical or judgemental considerations. He or she should also not be influenced by pressure from the client organization. The latter may seem a strange requirement, but consultants are employed specifically to take an independent view. It follows, therefore, that you should expect a consultant to disagree with some of your suggestions. This is actually a good sign and indicates that the problem is being viewed from a different and independent perspective.

What do consultants do?

The process of consultancy is often compared to the steps taken by a doctor to diagnose and treat a medical condition. Obviously the work undertaken by a business psychologist is seldom (if ever) of a life-or-death variety, but the medical analogy serves to highlight the method. Consider the following office equipment company case study.

Case study: The disappearing salesforce

A large office equipment company found that the annual turnover of its sales staff was in excess of 30 per cent. This placed a heavy burden on the HR function and also had a significant impact on training and productivity. To make matters worse, the personnel who were leaving were the better performers, and those that remained were mostly of average sales ability. The company found the situation particularly baffling because their rates of pay were extremely competitive and, in some cases, significantly better than their rivals. A firm of consultants was called in to discover why people were leaving and to suggest how to rectify the situation – or, at the very least, reduce the staff turnover rate.

The first step taken by the consultants was to clarify the nature and size of the problem. Was it true that there was a 30 per cent attrition rate? Were all the top performers leaving? If not, who else was going? When was this happening? Over what time period? Where were they going? Was it related to sales territory? And so on.

Next, the process moved on to the causes of the problem. Was it a matter of pay? (It didn't seem so.) Other benefits? Conditions of work? The way in which employees were inducted? Opportunities for development or promotion? The expectations of the company? The psychological profile of those recruited?

The third step involved selecting an appropriate form of assessment to isolate the causes of the problem. In this case, it was decided to explore the biographical details and personality profiles of those people who had left, and compare them to those that remained. This was possible because data was available from the application forms and personality questionnaires completed by all employees as part of their selection procedure.

A thorough analysis of the results of the third step revealed that there were distinct differences in terms of personality and personal style between the two groups. It was apparent that if nothing was done to modify both the initial selection process, and the support system for those already employed, the problem would probably continue. Indeed, in the long term, there was the distinct possibility that the situation could deteriorate significantly.

The fourth step concentrated on developing a new selection process that placed greater emphasis on identifying people who would respond to the organization's culture. Simultaneously a number of changes were made to the nature of the job and more flexible working patterns were introduced, linked to a modified commission payment system. The revised selection process acted as a way of filtering out 'short stayers', but at the same time increased the chances of retaining those with high sales potential.

This case study illustrates the classic evidence-based approach to consulting – one that progresses logically through a number of interlinked stages. Of course, not all assignments require a consultant to move through every stage, but this approach does provide a robust framework for approaching many different situations. Returning to the medical analogy the stages can be identified as:

- **Examination.** What are the characteristics of the problem?
- **Diagnosis.** What are the possible causes?
- **Assessment.** How can the problem be quantified?
- **Prognosis.** What will happen over time?
- **Treatment.** How can the problem be resolved?
- **Prevention.** How can future problems be prevented?

The project proposal

The last section looked at the logical progression of an assignment but, if you are considering using a consultant, the first phase includes the production of a proposal. This summarizes the initial discussions between the consultant and the client and proposes an overall plan of action. There is no fixed format or length for a proposal – 'simple' projects may be covered in no more than two or three pages – but a complete proposal should include the following sections:

■ **Current situation**
This part describes how the consultant was contacted and who he or she has talked to in the client organization. It also outlines the consultant's view of the current situation (which should confirm the information provided by the client) and briefly reviews any new insights.

■ **Proposals**
In this part a number of possible solutions to the 'problem' will be identified. These will be presented in general terms, with a discussion of the techniques or products required to implement them. In addition, the consultant will explain the role which the client has to play in the process and the nature of the resources which will be required from the client's organization. These will often include various paper-based, electronic or computer records and the cooperation of staff at all levels.

■ **Terms of reference**
Within this part of the proposal you will find details of what the consultant intends to do. The terms of reference provide a programme of timed activities and also indicate the 'milestones' within an assignment, or the ways in which progress can be checked. If a proposal is accepted, it is these indicators that can be used by the client to determine whether everything has been completed. Note that it is important for the client to manage the consultancy process and to ensure that there are sufficient meetings to monitor progress. Critically, there should be 'no surprises' and the consultant should always be able to explain exactly what is being done at each stage.

■ **Benefit analysis**
If possible, a proposal will state the benefits which will be gained from a particular intervention in financial terms. For example, figures may be presented which indicate the potential savings to be gained from reducing staff turnover or implementing a new development programme. In addition 'soft' benefits such as increased motivation, commitment or better communications may be described. These are obviously more notional in nature, and are certainly harder to quantify, but they still add to the complete benefit picture.

■ **Fees**
Here, the total consulting fee is stated. This will include a breakdown, in consultant days, of the time required to complete the assignment. There will also be details of any service-based taxes, such as value added tax (VAT), and the method of payment. For many assignments additional details will be provided on the costs of particular assessment materials, or services provided by organizations retained by the consultant.

■ **The consulting organization**
A full proposal provides background information on the consultancy firm. This often includes details of other clients and relevant projects, and sometimes short biographies of those selected to conduct the assignment. The consultant in charge of the assignment, or the person who is sometimes called the 'prime', should also be identified.

■ **Terms of business**
The final section concerns the conditions of the contract. These are often a standard set of points relating to issues such as the provision of consultants, hours of working, chargeable expenses, invoicing procedures, cancellation fees, intellectual copyright, confidentiality and professional indemnity.

How much will it cost?

A consultant calculates the fees for an assignment by estimating the total time required for its completion. This is usually based on a fixed rate per consultant day, plus charges for support staff and any materials required. However, it should be remembered that the total time includes both contact time with the client organization, and any periods spent working on the assignment in the office. The latter is often the most significant component, as much work is done 'behind the scenes'. On occasions clients will also find that they have to pay for travel time; charges for travel and accommodation will certainly be made for projects which are remote from the consultant's home base.

Other charging systems may be applied, depending on the nature of the work. If a client only wants a limited amount of advice then an hourly rate will be levied. As with other professions, the fee will reflect the professional knowledge and skill required to deal with the enquiry. Likewise, if a standard set of assessments is being used in a well understood context – graduate selection, for example – a fixed rate per candidate may be available. However, whatever the situation, the fees charged should be commensurate with the service provided. It is in no-one's interests, least of all the consultant's, to damage a client relationship by charging excessive fees.

It is also the case that no consultancy firm is likely to enter into an arrangement which only pays if there is a measurable outcome: a 'contingent fee' approach. This is because, while business psychology provides a number of very effective techniques, it cannot *guarantee* increases in productivity, greater profits or a reduction in costs. If it could, the 'no win–no fee' approach required would only work if there was some way of indemnifying firms against losses. It is interesting to note that a number of US consultancy firms are considering this approach, but only after securing safeguards similar to those found in the legal system.

In 1998 the typical fee for a consultant day in the UK ranged from about £400 to well over £1500. In the USA the comparable figure was $800 to $4000 a day. Although this makes consultancy look like an expensive option, if inflation is adjusted for, fees have not risen significantly since the 1960s. Thus the real question is: what is the cost-benefit?

Working out the benefits

One way of deciding whether it is worth changing your selection or assessment practices is to perform a utility analysis. This is an established method for calculating the benefit of a particular procedure. It takes into account the method used, the number of people in which 'improvements' are expected, and the fixed costs of the process. Put simply, the utility formula can be expressed as:

$$\text{Benefit} = (\text{Quality} \times \text{Quantity}) - \text{Cost}$$

The quality part of the equation is based on a number of factors. First is the validity of the procedure used. This is the correlation between the procedure and performance in the job – for example, the relationship between a test score and a measure of productivity. The second factor is the average performance of those selected using the procedure. This is derived from the standard score which would be obtained if the selection procedure was perfect, divided by the 'selection ratio', which is the proportion of applicants actually selected. Third is the difference, expressed as a proportion of yearly salary, between a good and average employee. In practice, this is usually taken as being equivalent to at least 40 per cent of the first year's salary. The total 'quality' figure is then found by multiplying these three factors together.

The quantity value is calculated by multiplying the number of candidates selected in a year, by the average number of years for which those candidates stay with the organization. Finally, all the administration and implementation costs are subtracted from the quality value, appropriately scaled by the quantity.

In practice, the utility equation can be applied to any form of selection or assessment procedure for which there is reliable validity information and, as the following case study illustrates, it can help reveal significant benefits – an important element in any situation where changes to HR practices need to be quantified in financial terms.

Case study: The graduate assessment centre

A national retail organization with 18 000 employees runs assessment centres for 200 graduate-level applicants each year. This entails using 20 assessment centres in order to select 40 managers earning £25 000 per annum. The organization calculates that it costs £1200 per candidate in administration costs to use the system. This takes into account the pre-screening of all the applicants with an application form, and the costs of the assessment centres which incorporate interviews, psychometric tests, presentations, and exercises which candidates perform in groups.

Before assessment centres were used, the organization selected graduates on the basis of interviews alone. Although these were cheaper, costing £350 per candidate, over a number of years it had been noticed that there was a wide variation in the performance of managers selected using this method. Hence the change to a system which provided a better assessment of candidates and was more predictive of future performance. It was also possible to demonstrate real financial benefits in using assessment centres over the previous approach, not least because 'better' graduates now stayed for an average of four years, whereas before they had left after only two.

Using the formula outlined earlier, the HR director responsible for the assessment centre programme was able to demonstrate the following gain for each set of 40 appointments:

Benefit = (validity of procedure × standard score × 40% of salary) multiplied by (number selected × average number of years in organization) subtract (total cost of selection procedure).

Benefit = $(0.4 \times 1.4 \times £10\,000) \times (40 \times 4) - (200 \times £1200) = £656\,000$

In comparison the calculation for using the 'cheaper', but less valid, interview was:

Benefit = $(0.2 \times 1.4 \times £10\,000) \times (40 \times 2) - (200 \times £350) = £154\,000$

Thus the actual gain over the original approach was £502 000 or £12 550 per successful appointment.

Note: For the technically minded, the validity figures are those which have been calculated in commercial settings for assessment centres and interviews respectively. The standard score is based on the selection ratio, which is one in five in this case, divided by the ordinate under the normal curve for that ratio. The latter is the standard score you would expect if the selection procedure is perfect and always selects the top 20 per cent but, of course, the selection procedure is never perfect and so that is why we multiply it by the validity.

The assessment centre example also demonstrates that the benefit is greatest when the validity of the selection procedure is high and the selection ratio is low. Thus it makes sense to use sophisticated procedures in those situations where there are a large number of applicants relative to the number of positions available. It is also particularly effective when there are significant variations in performance in the target job, or if the procedure is used to select those for senior, high salary jobs.

Using consultants

The techniques described in this book are the stock-in-trade of the business psychologist. However, as not all psychologists who consult on work-related issues will use the qualifier 'business', you should also look out for those who term themselves 'organizational', 'work', 'industrial', 'applied' or 'occupational' psychologists. Indeed, the relevant professional body in the UK, the British Psychological Society (BPS), maintains a separate 'Occupational' division which incorporates business psychologists.

If you decide to use the services provided by a consultant you should always check that he or she has the correct qualifications. This is important because, at present, anyone in the UK, whatever their background, may call themselves a 'psychologist'.

To help resolve the confusion the BPS publishes a Register of Chartered Psychologists. These are all people who have the necessary academic and professional qualifications to practise and, as with other professions, all those registered have also agreed to abide by a code of conduct, and to maintain and develop their professional competence.

You can easily check the credentials of any psychologist by consulting the Register or by contacting the BPS directly. In addition, it is useful to know that only Chartered Psychologists may use the abbreviation 'C.Psychol.' after their names, or the title 'Chartered Psychologist'. Those who specialize in particular areas may also qualify their titles by, for example, inserting the word 'Occupational'. This not only indicates that they consult in a particular area of psychology – in this case, business psychology – but that they have additional professional training and experience. Indeed, such psychologists are the only group of HR-oriented specialists to have a minimum of six years' degree and postgraduate training specifically aimed at understanding individuals in relation to the organization.

The Register not only contains details on occupational psychologists, but on clinical, counselling, educational and forensic specialists as well. Thus it acts as a comprehensive guide to the whole discipline. Indeed, some of the other types of psychologist listed also work in a business setting. For example, counselling and clinical psychologists may deal with workplace stress, individual development and employee counselling.

Thus when you are searching for a consultant the first point of reference is the Register. However, the BPS also publishes a *Directory of*

Chartered Psychologists. This is more like a version of the *Yellow Pages* and is the only comprehensive list of practising psychologists. It provides a guide to the sort of services offered, and a regional index. Those included in the *Directory* can also provide additional information on their professional interests, hours of work, languages spoken, and so on.

Having identified a suitably qualified consultant, or preferably two or three, you should refine your brief. Make sure that you know the extent of the project you have in mind, how much money you are prepared to spend, the way in which you wish the project to be managed, and how you will want to check on progress. Once you have decided on these issues you need to carry out a number of final checks. It is extremely important to assess how an individual or firm presents themselves and to decide who you could best work with. In short, is the 'chemistry' right and do you feel at ease? The following checklist will help.

- Is the first meeting thorough and professional?
- Do you feel comfortable asking questions?
- Can the consultant answer your concerns?
- Does the consultant actively listen to your needs?
- Are your requirements summarized accurately?
- Is plain English used or is there an excess of jargon?
- Does the consultant agree with everything you say? (Not a good sign!)
- Has the consultant (successfully) completed a similar project?
- What is the consultant's professional background?
- What sort of organization does the consultant work for?

Obviously you need to have confidence in a consultant's objectivity, which is one reason to be suspicious of someone who agrees with everything you say. Also, as the checklist suggests, you should enquire about similar projects, and ask for references from former clients, as appropriate, so that you can be assured that the consultant has dealt with organizations with comparable problems to your own. However, strictly speaking, a consultant need not have completed an identical project; he or she should be able to critically appraise your situation and present a range of informed proposals. Likewise, you should not necessarily dismiss consultants who work for themselves, or in small practices. Sometimes a genuinely independent practitioner may be preferable to a large consultancy which may present you with a large bill for merely mediocre work.

In fact, a smaller firm probably depends more on attracting sufficient work through referrals, and so will put considerable effort into maintaining the client relationship. This usually means that greater importance is attached to providing a more personal and focused service, which is no bad thing as you should be employing an individual or a close-knit team, not a bureaucracy.

In conclusion, select your consultants with care because you will have to live with the consequences of their actions. If you follow the advice given in this chapter you should be able to retain the services of a well qualified and professional consultant who is able to understand your requirements from a broad and objective perspective, independent of the internal power structure which colours the operation of all organizations.

Further information

British Psychological Society. *Directory of Chartered Psychologists* and *Register of Chartered Psychologists*, Leicester: BPS.

The Directory and Register can be consulted in all large UK reference libraries. They can also be purchased from:

The British Psychological Society, St Andrews House, 48 Princess Road East, Leicester, LE1 7DR, UK. Telephone: 0116 254 9568 Facsimile: 0116 247 0787.

Other useful contacts are:

Institute of Management Consultants, 5th Floor, 32–33 Hatton Garden, London EC1N 8DL. Telephone: 0171 242 1803 Facsimile: 0171 831 4597.

Institute of Personnel and Development, IPD House, Camp Road, Wimbledon, London SW19 4UX. Telephone: 0181 971 9000 Facsimile: 0181 879 7000.

In other countries contact the professional association for psychologists – for example, the American Psychological Association, the various European associations or, in Australasia, the Australian Psychological Society.

Afterword: The Challenge of Change

We trained hard but it seemed that every time we were beginning to form up in teams we would be reorganised. I was to learn later in life that we tend to meet any new situation by reorganising, and a wonderful method it can be for creating the illusion of progress while producing confusion, inefficiency and demoralisation.
(Caius Petronius, AD 65)

All the techniques described in this book can be used to change organizations. But change has many faces. Sometimes, as Petronius suggests, it can be an end in itself. Yet underlying the process are two great truths. Change, like it or not, is continuous. Just think how jobs have altered over the last 10–15 years. It is also something which is met with resistance. After all, it is much easier to continue with tried and tested methods, which may well be successful, than try something new.

It is the manager's job to smooth the passage of change, to allow people and systems to evolve, and to address the natural resistance to all change that exists. One very practical way of making the task easier is to always tackle the following points:

- **Schedule**. All change and development programmes need to be planned in detail. Objectives, timings, costs and responsibilities should be crystal clear. Crucially, senior executives must be seen to actively endorse and support the programme.
- **Set goals**. It is easier to monitor progress through the use of short-term goals or 'milestones'. Make sure that achievements are acknowledged and that the focus is on progressive and visible improvement, not 'buck-passing' or fault-finding. As such, goals must be explicit and quantifiable – for example, increase productivity by X per cent and decrease costs by Y per cent.
- **Prepare employees**. Whatever the purpose of a change programme, whether it be concerned with assessment or organizational development, employees must be fully briefed. Surprises seldom work well! In particular, ensure that meaningful two-way communication is established.
- **Check resistance**. If employees are briefed it will help to pre-empt any resistance. Make sure that everyone knows what is to be gained or lost by change. This requires a mechanism which allows the cascade of information to all levels.

■ **Involvement.** In most situations employees will be more supportive if they have been consulted on the content of a change programme. Involve as many employees as possible and create a climate of change – for example, move people out of their 'comfort zones' and create a sense of urgency.

■ **Integrate.** Many programmes will interact with organizational elements such as reward systems, lines of communication and other organizational structures. Make sure that the likely effects are known before any intervention and watch out for the inevitable knock-on effect from one system to another.

Finally be mindful that, despite the best preparations, there are often unpredictable outcomes. Be ready for the unexpected, as an organization prepared for uncertainty will be in a healthier position to capitalize on the opportunities which change delivers.

The changing workplace

Over the next few years organizations will need to respond to a number of powerful forces. These include globalization, consumerism and the changing nature of careers. To respond to the first of these requires a recognition of the fact that increasing numbers of businesses are operating in a global market and that this requires 24-hours-a-day activity. It also necessitates the development of new and quicker ways of doing business which, for many, will involve the use of advanced information systems and the Internet. This style of operation needs a technically adept, highly motivated and flexible workforce.

Consumerism acts at a national and international level and is driven by the shift in power from the producer to the consumer. A good illustration is the recent developments in the financial services industry, such as telephone banking, which are driven by consumer demand. Indeed, the growth of all forms of service industry, which often involve the sophisticated manipulation of large quantities of data, now account for a significant proportion of the economic output of most developed countries. Such activity is altering the fundamental structure of employment and confirms that the 'fourth wave' of work (agrarian, industrial, service, information) is indeed upon us.

Finally, as a result of many years of economic instability many are constructing a different type of career plan. The so-called 'portfolio' career is based on the assumption that no job is for life and that individuals are responsible for their own progress and development. This challenges the very concept of the 'employee', and, indeed, a number of organizations now claim to have no employees at all – just people who work with them towards a common goal. In this environment managers can help to broker the interface between job and career, through concepts such as the learning organization and the removal of artificial boundaries within jobs. Nevertheless, the effects of downsizing and increased competition still mean that many organizations will need to try much harder to retain their best employees. Paradoxically, this requires us to develop systems which make our colleagues become more employable!

The application of business psychology, and in particular a more enlightened view of personal development, represents the professional response to these trends. In short, the most important competency of all becomes the organization's ability to manage its relationship with its staff. This is essential to continuing prosperity and the only real source of differentiation between one business and another. The other differences, history tells us, are all too easy to duplicate.

Test Publishers and Consultancies

United Kingdom

Assessment for Selection and
Employment
Hanover House
2–4 Sheet Street
Windsor
Berkshire
SL4 1BG
Telephone: + 44 (0)1753 850333
Facsimile: + 44 (0)1753 620972

Belbin Associates
The Burleigh Business Centre
52 Burleigh Street
Cambridge
CB1 1DJ
Telephone: +44 (0)1223 360896
Facsimile: +44 (0)1223 368746

The Criterion Partnership
Churchward Court
15 Western Road
Lewes
East Sussex
BN7 1RL
Telephone: + 44 (0)1273 480583
Facsimile: + 44 (0)1273 487271

Development Dimensions
International Ltd
Keystone House
Boundary Road
Loudwater
High Wycombe

Buckinghamshire
HP10 9PY
Telephone: +44 (0)1628 810800
Facsimile: +44 (0)1628 810320

Hay Management Consultants
52 Grosvenor Gardens
London
SW1W 0AU
Telephone: +44 (0)171 730 0833
Facsimile: +44 (0)171 730 8193

KPMG Management Consulting
8 Salisbury Square
London
EC4Y 8BB
Telephone: +44 (0)171 311 8000
Facsimile: +44 (0)171 311 8274

The Morrisby Organisation
(formerly Educational and
Industrial Test Services Ltd)
83 High Street
Hemel Hempstead
Hertfordshire
HP1 3AH
Telephone: + 44 (0)1442 215521
Facsimile: + 44 (0)1442 240531

Oxford Psychologists Press Ltd
Lambourne House
311–321 Banbury Road
Oxford
OX2 7JH
Telephone: + 44 (0)1865 510203
Facsimile: + 44 (0)1865 310368

PA Consulting Group
123 Buckingham Palace Road
London
SW1W 9SR
Telephone: +44 (0)171 730 9000
Facsimile: +44 (0)171 333 5452

PE Consulting Ltd
Park House
Wick Road
Egham
Surrey
TW20 0HW
Telephone: +44 (0)1784 434411
Facsimile: +44(0)1784 471405

Price Waterhouse
Southwark Towers
32 London Bridge Street
London
SE1 9SY
Telephone: +44 (0)171 939 3000
Facsimile: +44 (0)171 378 0647

PRIcoa Relocation Management
136 New Bond Street
London
W1Y 0PB
Telephone: +44 (0)171 629 8222
Facsimile: +44 (0)171 499 4162

Psi-Press
54 High View Road
Guildford
Surrey
GU2 5RT
Telephone: +44 (0)1483 567606
Facsimile: +44 (0)1483 456239

The Psychological Corporation
24–28 Oval Road
London
NW1 7DX
Telephone: + 44 (0)171 267 4466
Facsimile: + 44 (0)171 482 2293

Psytech International Ltd
The Grange
Church Road
Pullox Hill
Bedfordshire
MK45 5HE
Telephone: + 44 (0)1525 720003
Facsimile: + 44 (0)1525 720004

Saville & Holdsworth Ltd
3 AC Court
High Street
Thames Ditton
Surrey
KT7 0SR
Telephone: + 44 (0)181 398 4170
Facsimile: + 44 (0)181 398 9544

The Test Agency Ltd
Cray House
Woodlands Road
Henley-on-Thames
Oxfordshire
RG9 4AE
Telephone: + 44 (0)1491 413413
Facsimile: + 44 (0)1491 572249

TMS(UK) Ltd
Water Meadows
367 Huntington Road
York
YO3 9HR
Telephone: +44 (0)1904 641640
Facsimile: +44 (0)1904 640076

Worldwide

Australia
Australian Council for Educational
Research
19 Prospect Hill Road
Camberwell
Victoria
3124
Telephone: + 61 3 9277 5555
Facsimile: + 61 3 9277 5500

PsytechPress
Level 4
398 Lonsdale Street
Melbourne
Victoria
Telephone: + 61 3 9670 0590
Facsimile: + 61 3 9642 3577

Canada
Institute of Psychological
Research, Inc.
34 Fleury Street West
Montreal
Quebec
H3L 159
Telephone: + 1 514 382 3000
Facsimile: + 1 514 382 3007

Denmark
Dansk Psykologisk Forlag
Stockholmsgade 29
DK-2100 Copenhagen
Denmark
Telephone: + 45 31 381 655
Facsimile: + 45 31 381 665

Eire
ETCC
17 Leeson Park
Dublin 6
Telephone: + 353 14 972067
Facsimile: + 353 14 972518

France
Editions du Centre de Psychologie
Appliquée
25 rue de la Plaine
75980 Paris
Cedex 20
Telephone: + 33 1 4009 6262
Facsimile: + 33 1 4009 6280

Germany
Hogrefe-Verlag fur Psychologie
Rohnsweg 25

Postfach 3751
D-37085 Gottingen
Telephone: + 49 551 49609 0
Facsimile: + 49 551 49609 88

Hong Kong
Transglobal Publishers Services Ltd
27/F Unit E
Shield Industrial Centre
84/92 Chai Wan Kok Street
Tsuen Wan, NT
Telephone: + 852 2413 5322
Facsimile: + 852 2413 7049

India
Manasayan
Agarwal Complex
S-524, School Block
Shakarpur
Delhi 110092
Telephone: + 91 11 222 3919
Facsimile: + 91 11 327 1584

Israel
Ramot of Tel Aviv University
32 Haim Levanon Street
Ramit-Aviv
Tel-Aviv 61392
Telephone: + 972 3 642 6465
Facsimile: + 972 3 642 9865

Italy
Organizzazioni Speciali
Via Fra'Paolo Sarpi, 7/A
50136 Firenze
Telephone: + 39 55 672580
Facsimile: + 39 55 669446

Japan
Nihon Bunka Kagakusha
Honkonagome 6-15-17
Bunkyo-Ku
Tokyo 113
Telephone: + 81 3 3946 3131
Facsimile: + 81 3 3946 3567

Netherlands
Swets Test Services
Heerewag 347b
PO Box 820
2160 SZ Lisse
Telephone: + 312 524 35375
Facsimile: + 312 524 15888

New Zealand
New Zealand Council for
Educational Research
Education House
178–182 Willis Street
Wellington 1
Telephone: + 64 43 847939
Facsimile: + 64 43 847933

Norway
Norsk Psykologforening
Storgaten 10a
N-0155 Oslo
Telephone: + 47 22 42 1980
Facsimile: + 47 22 42 4292

Portugal
Psico
Rua Luis Pastor de Macedo
Lote 29
1700 Lisbon
Telephone: + 351 1 758 6795
Facsimile: + 351 1 759 8891

Singapore
Nelson Publishers
105 Sims Avenue #07-12
Chancerlodge Complex
Singapore 1438
Telephone: + 65 747 2512
Facsimile: + 65 744 3318

South Africa
Impact Careers Assessments (Pty)
Ltd
17th Floor
Noswell Hall

Cnr Jan Smuts Ave & Stiemens
Street
Braamfontein
Johannesburg
Telephone: + 27 11 4037200
Facsimile: + 27 11 4032584

Spain
TEA Ediciones, SA
Fray Bernardino de Sahagun 24
Madrid 28036
Telephone: + 34 1 359 8311
Facsimile: + 34 1 345 8608

Sweden
Psykologiforlaget AB
Box 47054
S-10074 Stockholm
Telephone: + 46 8 681 0000
Facsimile: + 46 8 681 0002

Turkey
Institute for Behavioral Studies
Dumen S. Gumus Palas
Apt. No: 1/10
Kat: 3 Gumussayu-Taksim
80090 Istanbul
Telephone: + 90 212 293 9339
Facsimile: + 90 212 243 4472

United States of America
Centre for Creative Leadership
PO Box 26300
Greensboro
NC 27438-6300
Telephone: + 1 336 545 2810
Facsimile: + 1 336 282 3284

Consulting Psychologists Press, Inc.
577 College Avenue
PO Box 60070
Palo Alto
California
94306
Telephone: + 1 800 624 1765
Facsimile: + 1 650 969 8608

McGraw-Hill
London House
9701 W. Higgins Road
Rosemont
Illinois
Telephone: + 1 800 221 8378
Facsimile: + 1 708 292 3400

Institute of Personality and Ability
Testing, Inc.
1801 Woodfield Drive
Savoy
Illinois
61874
Telephone: + 1 217 352 4739
Facsimile: + 1 217 352 9674

Psychological Assessment
Resources, Inc.
PO Box 998
Odessa
Florida
33556
Telephone: + 1 813 968 3003
Facsimile: + 1 813 968 2598

Purdue Research Foundation
(PAQ)
1625 North 1000 East
North Logan
Utah
84341
Telephone: + 1 801 752 5698
Facsimile: + 1 801 752 5712

Glossary

Ability test   A test which objectively measures the ability to perform a certain task – for example, the ability to reason with verbal problems.

Adverse impact   The result of applying a selection criterion (for example, a test cut-off score) which results in fewer members of a particular minority, gender or ethnic group meeting the criterion.

Aptitude test   A test which is designed to measure potential performance, or how someone is likely to perform in the future.

Assessment centre   An integrated selection procedure which involves the use of a range of techniques such as psychometric tests, interviews and group exercises. Candidates are generally assessed across a range of tasks by a number of trained assessors.

Attainment test   A test which measures what a person already knows in terms of knowledge or skills.

Behaviourally anchored rating scale (BARS)   Scales which are used to rate behaviour against a fixed set of indicators.

Behavioural interview   An interview based on a series of questions which relate to abilities in particular job-related activities. Sometimes called the criterion-referenced interview

Belbin's team roles   A categorization of team behaviour devised by Meredith Belbin. His latest typology is based on nine team roles. For example, the two leadership roles are those of the 'coordinator' and the 'shaper'.

Benchmarking   The process of comparing work performance against an external measure of best practice.

'Big five'   Many personality questionnaires can be defined in terms of five main dimensions – the so-called 'Big Five'. These are extroversion, tough-mindedness, anxiety, independence and individual organization.

Biodata   A system of assessment which profiles a candidate against statistical meaningful biographical data. For example, an analysis of current job-holders may reveal that the best performers are those with a certain type of previous employment experience or particular job-specific qualifications.

Biodata form   A structured application form which allows candidates to be scored against the requirements for a job.

Biographical interview   The 'traditional' interview which asks candidates about their previous work experience, educational history, interests, background and aspirations.

Bottom-up selection   A selection procedure which involves setting a minimum level of performance as a cut-off score; candidates who exceed this level pass on to the next method of assessment, usually an interview.

Business learning exercise   A form of assessment which is based on a complete problem scenario. Candidates are led through a series of tasks which teach them what to do; they then have to apply this learning to a further series of tasks.

Chartered psychologist   A psychologist who holds a first degree in Psychology (or its equivalent) who has undergone a further period of training or study lasting at least three years.

Competency   A term used for a cluster of factors, including abilities, personality, skills, knowledge and experience, which are predictive of performance. For example, the competencies 'persuasiveness' and 'negotiation skill' are predictive of sales performance.

Competency framework   A system of job classification based on a complete definition of a job, or jobs, in terms of competencies.

Construct   A term used to describe the way in which a person filters information. We each devise unique construct systems which allow us to make sense of the world around us. See **repertory grid technique**.

Correlation   A measure of the relationship between two variables. For example, there is a positive relationship between age and knowledge – that is, the older you are, the more you know.

Counselling   In the workplace, counselling refers to the process of helping employees understand the problems which face them and enabling them to devise practical solutions. See **employee assistance programmes**.

Criterion measure   A measure of a particular aspect of performance. These can include appraisal ratings, examination results, or performance as measured by (another) psychometric test.

Critical incident technique   A job analysis technique which is designed to uncover examples of behaviour that have had a significant effect on work performance, both good and bad.

Cut-off score   A fixed test score used to decide whether a candidate has 'passed' or 'failed'.

Development centre   An assessment centre used within an organization for internal development and training.

Direct discrimination   The action of treating people less favourably because they belong to particular minority, gender or ethnic groups.

Employee assistance programme   A confidential counselling service offered to employees, designed to counter the work- and home-related problems which affect work performance.

Eustress   Positive stress which leads to an improvement in efficiency and performance.

Face validity   A term used to describe any form of assessment which looks as though it is measuring what it is supposed to measure. Note that this does not mean that the assessment actually works!

Feedback   The process of telling a candidate how he or she has performed on a test. 360-degree feedback is a technique which gathers information on an individual from himself or herself *and* colleagues, subordinates and bosses.

Focus group   An organized discussion forum. Focus groups are often used in job analysis to clarify the purpose, behaviours and actions required to perform particular jobs.

Group exercise   A form of assessment in which a group of candidates have to work together on a specific problem. Such exercises can include discussion tasks or practical activities like bridge-building.

Impression management   The tendency for candidates to place the best possible spin on their abilities or personality. For example, candidates may manipulate their responses to a personality questionnaire in order to maximize their chances of fulfilling the requirements for a job. This form of behaviour is also known as motivational distortion.

In-tray exercise   A practical assessment exercise which is designed to mimic the administrative aspects of a job.

Indirect discrimination   A selection requirement which has the effect of unjustifiably discriminating against members of a particular minority, gender or ethnic group.

Interests questionnaire   A self-report questionnaire which asks about employment or work interests

Ipsative   An approach to test design and interpretation which allows a range of personal attributes to be directly compared with one another – for example, a design which allows the relative strengths of a range of abilities to be explored, independent of the absolute level of the scores obtained.

Item   Another name for the questions in a test or questionnaire.

Job analysis   The process of systematically examining the tasks which make up a particular job, and the abilities, knowledge, skills and experience required to perform them.

Job description   A report, based on a job analysis, which describes the tasks involved in a particular job, the performance criteria and areas of control and responsibility.

Job evaluation   The formal process of assessing jobs in order to calculate pay rates.

Learning organization   An organizational culture which promotes individual learning as a continuous process.

Learning style   An individual's preferred way(s) of learning.

Mastery test   A test in which there are only two outcomes – pass or fail. Examples of mastery tests are professional examinations and the driving test.

Motivation questionnaire   A form of questionnaire which is designed to discover what motivates individuals. For instance, most questionnaires measure aspects of energy (for example, competition), synergy (for example, recognition), intrinsic factors (for example, autonomy) and extrinsic factors (for example, status).

Narrative report   The expression used to describe a report which has been generated by an expert computer test interpretation system.

Normal curve   The bell-shaped curve which is obtained if the frequency of a continuous behavioural attribute is plotted. For instance, if basic arithmetical ability was assessed in the general population, most people would score, by definition, in the average range, with progressively fewer above or below average.

Normative group   A large representative sample of the population against which a candidate's test performance can be compared. Commonly used norm groups are those based on data from people of particular ages, the general UK population and 'occupational' groups, such as managers.

Normative comparison   The expression used when comparing the test results of a candidate against a suitable norm group.

Outplacement   The process of systematically placing employees in new jobs or training after they have been made redundant.

Percentile   The position of a candidate's test score in comparison to the percentage of values in the norm group falling above or below that score. For example, if a score was at the 90th percentile that would place it in the top 10 per cent of the population.

Person specification   A description of the essential abilities, skills, knowledge, experience and other characteristics which are required to perform a particular job.

Personality questionnaire   A self-report questionnaire which looks at aspects of typical behaviour – for example, how a person usually interacts with other people (relating), how he or she approaches tasks (action), and how he or she feels (feeling/anxiety).

Practice test   A short self-explanatory version of a test which is sent to a candidate before a test session. It provides information on what is being measured and some practice items to complete.

Predictive validity   This concerns whether or not a test or some other form of assessment predicts future work performance.

Psychometric profile   A profile of a candidate's abilities and personality which can be matched against a person specification. It is also the basis of using test results in an **ipsative** manner.

Psychometric test   A standard way of assessing a specific aspect of behaviour. Effective tests must also be reliable and valid. See **reliability** and **validity**.

Raw score   The number of test items answered correctly, or the score on a particular scale in a personality or interests questionnaire.

Reliability   How consistent a test is in itself, whether items within a test correlate with each other, and how stable it is across time.

Repertory grid technique   A form of interview in which a person is asked to systematically compare a series of job-related elements (for example, work activities) in order to uncover his or her personal construct system. In a job analysis the constructs might concern the individual attributes required to perform the activities. See **constructs**.

Role play   A type of assessment in which a candidate has to respond to an assessor playing a part. For example, the candidate may have to deal with a 'difficult' customer.

Scale score   A standardized raw score.

Selection ratio   The ratio of those selected for a job to the total number of applicants.

Situational interview   An interview in which a candidate has to respond, using one of a number of given answers, to a work-related scenario. The responses will have been previously rated by job incumbents for their suitability.

Standard error of measurement   A statistic which indicates the accuracy of test scores.

Standardization   The process of producing a representative set of test norms.

Stressor   A factor in an employee's work or home life that has become a source of stress – for example, working excessive hours or interpersonal problems.

Tailored test   A test specially written for a client to assess the requirements of a specific job.

Test–retest reliability   The process of delivering a test to the same set of candidates on two different occasions in order to check whether or not it gives the same results.

Top-down selection   A selection procedure which involves selecting those with the highest test scores.

Training needs analysis   An analytic technique used to assess the training requirements of an organization in light of its policy towards personal development and strategic aims.

Trainability test   A test designed to discover how quickly a candidate can learn a particular task.

Trait   A specific aspect of personality – for example, virtually all personality questionnaires measure the trait 'extroversion'.

Trialling   The process of 'testing' a test to make sure that it is fair, reliable and valid. Trials are also used to develop normative data.

Utility   The average gain in productivity per employee of using one sort of assessment (for example, a test) as compared to an alternative form of selection (for example, an interview).

Validity   This concerns the accuracy of a test or the degree to which it measures what it is supposed to measure – for example, the degree to which a numerical test actually measures numerical ability and is predictive of future numerical performance.

Virtual team   A team which is managed and performs its business with the minimum of physical contact. Teams of this sort usually communicate through computer-based systems.

Visionary interview   An open-ended interview designed to reveal the future demands of a job.

Work profiling   A questionnaire-based method of job analysis.

Work sample test   A test which is based on specific aspects of a job – for example, a typing test which measures keyboard skills and the ability to produce error-free work.

Index